Adventure Guide™ *to the*

Cayman
Islands

Adventure Guide™ *to the*

Cayman Islands

Paris Permenter & John Bigley

HUNTER

HUNTER PUBLISHING, INC.
130 Campus Drive, Edison NJ 08818-7816, USA
Tel (732) 225 1900; Fax (732) 417 1744
E-mail: hunterpub@emi.net
Web site: www.hunterpublishing.com

1220 Nicholson Road, Newmarket
Ontario L3Y 7V1, CANADA
Tel (800) 399 6858; Fax (800) 363 2665

ISBN 1-55650-786-0

Check Out Our Web Site!

For complete information about the hundreds of other travel guides and language courses offered by Hunter Publishing, visit us online at:
www.hunterpublishing.com

Cover Photo: Index Stock Photography
Page 13, courtesy of Lauren Bigley;
Photo credits: Page 56, courtesy of PT & Co.;
Page 110, courtesy of Atlantis Submarine;
all other images, Paris Permenter & John Bigley.
Maps by John Cotter Cartography.

1   2   3

Acknowledgments

We would like to thank those who helped on the homefront during our many research trips. Our thanks go to Laurie and Tim Kibel, Cliff and Clara Trahan, Sam Bertron and Rebecca Lowe for all their help. As always, special thanks to Mom and Dad for their support as we hit the road. Thanks to John Cotter for his professional map-making skills.

Thanks also go to our daughter, Lauren Bigley, who traveled with us on many research trips and helped give us the perspective of a first-time visitor to the Cayman Islands.

Our research was also assisted by the many public relations agencies across the country; their hard work made our jobs much easier. Special thanks go to Patrice Tanaka & Company, Cheryl Andrews Marketing, Karen Weiner Escalera Associates, Leone & Leone, and especially the Cayman Islands Department of Tourism.

About The Authors

John Bigley and Paris Permenter are professional travel writers and photographers specializing in the Caribbean. The team contribute travel articles and photographs to many top magazines and newspapers.

Paris and John are the authors of *Adventure Guide to the Leeward Islands*, also by Hunter Publishing. The couple have authored *Caribbean for Lovers, Gourmet Getaways: A Taste of North America's Top Resorts, Texas Getaways for Two, Day Trips from San Antonio and Austin, The Alamo City Guide*, and *Texas Barbecue*, named Best Regional Book by the Mid-America Publishers Assoc. The couple are frequent TV and radio talk show guests and have appeared on several travel shows. Both Paris and John are members of the prestigious Society of American Travel Writers (SATW) and the American Society of Journalists and Authors (ASJA). The husband-wife team reside in the Texas Hill Country near Austin.

Contents

Charts

The Cayman Islands

Maps

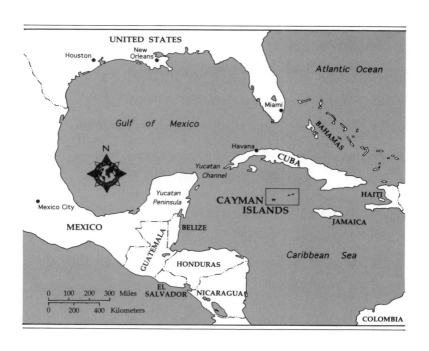

The Cayman Islands

Introduction

Once a few isolated islands populated by just a handful of residents, today the Cayman Islands garner the attention of both the travel and the business world. These islands are straight out of "Lifestyles of the Rich and Famous," the kind of destination where businesspeople might take care of banking chores in the morning and scuba dive in the afternoon. Have a good look around at the sunglasses-clad fellow on the next chaise longue. He may well be in the islands to visit his bulging, tax-free bank account. Two bikinis down, that may be a New York model taking a break from the workaday world or a businesswoman on-island to attend a board of directors meeting of an offshore insurance company.

For travelers, these islands are a destination sought for their underwater attractions, boasting many of the best dive sites on the globe, waters with a clarity second to none, a diversity of dives to interest even the most jaded diver, and a variety of marine life that can't be beat. Vacations here center around those crystalline waters. Divers and snorkelers will find marine playgrounds around each of the islands. Fishermen wrestle with wily bonefish in the shallow flats or struggle with blue marlin, yellowfin tuna, or wahoo from deepwater charter boats. Those looking for a more leisurely pace enjoy sunset sails or long walks along powdery sand beaches.

Business travelers frequent the largest of the three Cayman Islands, Grand Cayman. Unlike many Caribbean islands, whose commerce is concentrated in inter-island trade, Grand Cayman is a major player in the world market. This tiny isle is the fifth largest financial center in the world, with over 500 banks. More than 30,000 businesses are incorporated here, most of them nothing more than a plaque on a wall somewhere. The reason for the island's position as a business capital is its banking and trust laws and tax-free status. (Remember *The Firm*? Portions of that movie, based on the

John Grisham book, were filmed right here and based on the island's banking secrecy laws.)

The affluence brought about by its position as a financial leader has both pros and cons for the vacationer. On one hand, you'll find the Cayman Islands are a safe destination, a place where you can walk on the beach, drive around in an open-air jeep, and exercise no more than common-sense safety precautions. You will never be bothered by beach hasslers trying to hawk jewelry or braid your hair, something many vacationers resent on other Caribbean islands. And you won't feel a sense of guilt staying in a luxurious hotel while local residents live in poverty, a problem in neighboring Jamaica.

For the American traveler, perhaps no other Caribbean islands offer the creature comforts and the feeling of being at "a home away from home" found here. This is especially true of Grand Cayman. This island, together with its smaller cousins, Cayman Brac and Little Cayman, enjoys the highest per capita income in the Caribbean. It is friendly, safe, and tailor-made for vacationers. Here you'll find all the comforts of the US, as well as an American standard of service in many restaurants, bars, and hotels. The islands' atmosphere is due largely to the many stateside expats who make their home here.

On the other hand, all this security and comfort comes at a price, and a steep one at that. When you step off the plane, 20% of your dollar is lost in the exchange rate. You'll be met by price tags that would be expensive if paid with a fully valued dollar; in paying with a dollar now worth only 80¢, you may find yourself gasping at some figures. There are ways to save money and do Cayman on just about any budget, though, and this book will help make your dollar go as far as possible.

This guide will also help you select the island and the activities right for you. The three islands, although similar in terrain, flora, and fauna, are vastly different in atmosphere. None of the Cayman Islands offers a rollicking experience of around-the-clock excitement, casino action, or frenetic shopping; travelers head to other islands for those experiences. But if you're looking for luxurious resorts, seaside golf, a little nightlife, and a somewhat party atmosphere, Grand Cayman is the place for you. Here, a plethora of watersports operators offer every type of water adventure you could wish for, restaurants and bars line busy Seven Mile Beach, and vacationers from around the globe fill hotels, condominiums, time shares, motels, and accommodations to suit most budgets. The largest of the three islands, Grand Cayman offers several types of experiences, from fun-loving Seven Mile Beach to quiet, little-changed East End and historic George Town.

If you're looking for seclusion, a real getaway, head to the Sister Islands: Little Cayman and Cayman Brac. These islands are true hideaways. You'll find dive operators, fishing guides, and charter boats on these tiny isles, as well as adventure around every bend.

Understand that whatever your choice, you're never limited to just one destination in the Cayman Islands. These isles are much smaller than their easterly neighbors, such as Cuba and Jamaica. You do not need to choose only one area or even one island for your vacation.

Grand Cayman visitors find that they can easily maneuver the entire landmass in one day. The island is shaped somewhat like a wrench, lying on its side with the jaws facing upwards, or north. The handle of the wrench is the East End. A main road circles the entire island, running east from George Town, tracing the shoreline as it snakes through small communities such as Bodden Town and Spotts. This road turns north at the end of the island and begins to trace the northern edge of the island, but you can take a shortcut halfway down the island on the Frank Sound Road, the route to the Queen Elizabeth II Botanic Gardens. When this road comes out on the north side, it travels west to Rum Point, a popular destination with vacationers who arrive by ferry from Seven Mile Beach and enjoy a day of fun in the sun. South of Rum Point, Cayman Kai is a quiet residential area filled with beautiful, expensive homes, and some untouched land that's still good for birding.

Rum Point and Cayman Kai look west across a vast, shallow body of water called the North Sound. Picturing the wrench, this body of water lies between the wrench's open jaws. Where this body of water meets the sea is the home of Stingray City, a must-do for any Cayman visitor, diver or not. Read more about Grand Cayman's top attraction in the East End section of this book.

Returning to the wrench, picture the top jaw of the tool. As it turns away from the handle, this is the location of George Town, the capital of the Cayman Islands and home of the international airport. Most visitors begin their vacation in this clean, orderly community.

From George Town, Seven Mile Beach sprawls to the north, tucked between the sea and the North Sound. This narrow strip of land may be small but it's not short on accommodations and restaurants; this is the heart of vacationland. Finally, Seven Mile Beach ends in West Bay, the clump of land on the westernmost side of the North Sound.

And while Grand Cayman offers plenty of activity for even the most action-packed vacation, don't feel you're bound by this 76-square-mile island. It's a short hop from George Town to either of the Sister Islands for an overnight stay or just a day trip. Also, inter-island flights connect Little Cayman and Cayman Brac, so you can, on any given day, do a little island-hopping for a totally different experience.

The choice is yours.

History

Cayman Brac and Little Cayman were spotted by Christopher Columbus during his last journey to the New World on May 10, 1503. Actually on his way from Panama to Hispaniola (now home of the Dominican Republic and Haiti), Columbus was blown off course, a detour that allowed him to sight the Sister Islands. He called these islands "Las Tortugas" after the many sea turtles he found there. In his notes, the explorer wrote " ...we were in sight of two very small islands, full of tortoises, as was the sea about, inasmuch as they looked like little rocks."

Later maps referred to the islands as Lagartos, probably a reference to the large lizards (possibly iguanas) seen on the island. Later, the name became Caymanas from the Carib Indian word for caymans, the marine crocodile. On a 1585 voyage, Sir Francis Drake reported sighting "great serpents called Caymanas, large like lizards, which are edible." A few years later, a French map showed Cayman Brac with crocodiles in its waters, along with a manuscript that described the reptiles. No modern residents had ever seen the toothy lizards, but in 1993 an archeological dig on Grand Cayman (and three years later on Cayman Brac) proved the existence of the crocodiles. But it was the turtle that continued to bring sailors to this region. To stave off scurvy, ships sailed to the island, then slaughtered and salted the turtles. For years, the isles served only as a pit stop on these maritime runs.

In 1655 the islands came under British control when Jamaica was captured from the Spanish by Oliver Cromwell's army. Tucked near Jamaica and Spanish-ruled Cuba, the British thought that the Cayman Islands were strategically located. According to legend, some deserters from Cromwell's army fled Jamaica with escaped slaves and arrived in Cayman Brac and Little Cayman in 1658. Allegedly, their names were Watler and Bowden, and today some of those islands' oldest families, the Watlers and the Boddens, may be their descendants. The possession of the islands by the British Empire wouldn't be official until 1670, when they were ceded to Britain along with Jamaica by the Treaty of Madrid. The Brits tried to settle the formerly uninhabited island of Grand Cayman, but continual problems with Spanish pirates sent the settlers back to Jamaica just a year later.

Slowly, the population increased and the first royal land grant in Grand Cayman came in 1734, marking the first permanent settlement. Through 1800, the island continued to grow in population with the arrival of shipwrecked mariners and immigrants from Jamaica. Cayman Brac and Little Cayman remained primarily uninhabited (some records show the tiny islands were settled but residents were attacked by pirates), only visited by turtle hunters during season.

For years, the Cayman Islands served as a magnet for pirates, and buccaneers such as Sir Henry Morgan enjoyed their sunny shores for at least brief stopovers. During the American Revolution, American privateers challenged English shipping, aided by the war ships and merchant ships of France, Spain, and Holland. By 1782, peace came to the seas and buccaneering drew to a close.

In 1832 the citizens of the Cayman Islands met at what is today the oldest remaining structure on the island, St. James Castle. Remembered as the "Birthplace of Democracy" in Cayman, this site witnessed the first vote to create a legislature of representatives.

THE WRECK OF TEN SAILS

According to the latest research, in 1794, a great maritime tragedy took place on the East End of Grand Cayman. "The Wreck of the Ten Sails" is still legendary on Grand Cayman, recalling the tragedy of the *Cordelia*, part of a convoy of merchant ships headed to Britain from Jamaica. *Cordelia* ran aground on the reef at the East End and frantically sent a signal to other ships to warn them off the dangerous coral. Sadly, the signal was misunderstood and, one by one, they all ran into the reef. Residents of East End were credited with their quick actions that left no life unsaved, an act that King George III later recognized. Various stories explain that King George III granted the islands freedom from conscription and other versions say that the king gave the islands freedom from taxation.

By 1835, slavery had been outlawed by Great Britain and the islands led a quiet existence, many of the population working as fishermen or building turtling boats. The sea provided a livelihood for most residents, who then traded for agricultural items that couldn't be grown on the island. Palm thatch was transformed into marine rope and offered a good barter for daily staples. During this time, shipbuilding became a major industry as well.

For the next century, the Cayman Islands remained relatively isolated. Residents continued their old traditions, but hurricanes, tidal waves, and a depletion of the green turtle supply forced some residents to sail to Cuba, Honduras, and Nicaragua to earn a living. The merchant seamen navigated the waters and this sustained the economy of the islands until tourism and finance rose to prominence in the 20th century. During this time, the islands were not only cut off geographically, but they also lacked much communication with the outside world. The first wireless station wasn't built until 1935.

The plunge into the 20th century was aided by commissioner Sir Allen Cardinall, who served on the island from 1934 to 1940. Linking the public buildings of Grand Cayman with a network of roads, the commissioner was also the first public figure to recognize the tourism potential of the islands, even noting that one beach was "the most perfect bathing beach in the West Indies."

In 1953, the first airfield in the Cayman Islands was completed – the Owens Roberts Airport on Grand Cayman. A year later, an airstrip opened on Cayman Brac. Within three years tourism began taking hold on Seven Mile Beach. By 1957, dive operator Bob Soto began the islands' first recreational diving business and introduced the world to these pristine waters.

The islands continued as a dependency of Jamaica, with both as protectorates of Great Britain until 1962 when Jamaica became independent. The Caymanians had a far different view of the Union Jack than their Jamaican neighbors, however; in 1962 a vote overwhelmingly favored the islands' remaining a British dependency.

TIMELINE

1503	Discovery by Christopher Columbus
1670	Islands ceded to Britain (along with Jamaica) under the Treaty of Madrid
1672	First settlers arrived near Bodden Town
1708	Great Britain renamed islands Cayman Islands
1835	Emancipation of slaves
1954	First airfield
1957	First recreational diving business
1962	Cayman Islands vote to remain British Crown Colony

Geography/Land

Located in the westernmost reaches of the Caribbean, Grand Cayman is about 180 miles west of Jamaica and 150 miles south of Cuba. It spans 76 square miles, approximately 22 miles long and eight miles at its widest point. The Sister Islands of Cayman Brac and Little Cayman are 80 miles east-northeast of Grand Cayman and are separated from each other by seven miles of ocean. Cayman

Brac covers about 14 square miles and Little Cayman, 10 square miles.

The three islands are similar, but not identical, in their landforms. Grand Cayman is irregularly shaped and includes the North Sound, a shallow bay of about 35 square miles. The elevation is low (about 60 feet above sea level at its highest point). The Sister Islands are each amoeba-shaped and small. Cayman Brac, about 12 miles long and a little over a mile wide, rises highest. The Bluff, from which the island gets its name (Brac is Gaelic for bluff), soars to a nosebleed level – by Caymanian standards – of 140 feet above sea level. This cliff falls into the sea and is one of the most picturesque features of the islands. A few miles west, Little Cayman is the flattest of the three islands, reaching just 40 feet above sea level in the middle of the island.

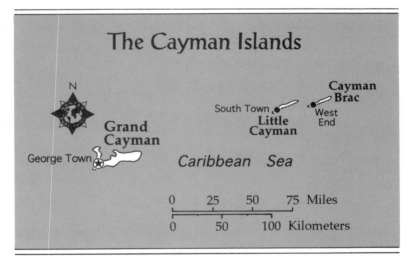

These three islands are the peaks of a submerged mountain range, Cayman Ridge, part of a chain running from Cuba to near Belize. The islands are actually limestone outcroppings with little soil, so vegetation is not as lush as that found on other Caribbean islands.

Two types of limestone form most of the surface: bluff limestone, formed about 30 million years ago, and ironshore, a substance created about 120,000 years ago, combining limestone with coral, mollusk shell, and marl. Ironshore accounts for the pocked surface that holds little pockets of soil (and makes walking barefoot just about impossible) on much of the islands.

The limestone is very porous, so most rain is quickly absorbed and the islands have no rivers or streams. That means little runoff and therefore greater clarity in the surrounding waters. Divers rave about the visibility, often 100 to 150 feet. Beyond the reaches of land, each island is surrounded by coral reefs, producing some of the best snorkeling and scuba diving in the Caribbean. Divers have a chance at spotting a wide array of marine life, partly because of the deep water located nearby. The Cayman Trough, the deepest water in the Caribbean, lies between this nation and Jamaica, with depths that plunge over four miles into inky blackness.

NOTE: *All beaches in the Cayman Islands are public.*

Climate

Blessed with cooling tradewinds, the Cayman Islands enjoy a temperate climate year-round. The hottest months are July and August when average temperatures top out at 85 to 90°; the coolest month is February, when highs range from 72 to 86° and nighttime lows dip to the mid-60s to lower 70s.

Water temperatures drop during the winter months, ranging from 78 to 82°. During the summer, the waters warm to 82-86°, a balmy bath-like temperature that makes wetsuits strictly optional.

Rainfall varies with the season, reaching its peak during hurricane season. Average rainfall is 46 inches annually; May and October are traditionally the wettest months. The driest times are March and April.

Mention weather and the Caribbean in the same sentence and, quite predictably, the topic of hurricanes arises. These deadly storms are officially a threat from June through November, although the greatest danger is during the later months, basically August through October. (September is the worst.)

Hurricanes are defined as revolving storms with wind speeds of 75 mph or greater. These counter-clockwise storms begin as waves off the west coast of Africa and work their way across the Atlantic, some eventually gaining strength and becoming tropical depressions (under 40 mph) or tropical storms (40-74 mph). Excellent warning systems keep islands posted on the possibility of oncoming storms. Radio Cayman (105.3 and 89.9) broadcasts current storm reports in the islands.

You'll find a list of hurricane shelters in the Cable and Wireless telephone directory. Keep in mind, however, that the Caribbean is a large region. We were on Grand Cayman when Hurricane Luis picked up strength on its way to batter St. Martin and Antigua in 1995, but we never saw surf over our ankles.

For a current weather report, call the **Cayman Islands National Meteorological Service** in George Town at ☎ (345) 945-5773 or check the weather page on the islands' Web site (www.caymans.com).

Flora & Fauna

Plant Life

The Cayman Islands are not as lush as neighboring Jamaica, but still boast a good variety of tropical flora and fauna. Since the islands were relatively isolated for centuries, residents became expert in the use of native flora for medicinal purposes. Some former uses of endemic plants included: coconut water to relieve kidney problems; mulberry and almond leaves applied externally for the treatment of rheumatism; aloe to relieve burns and rashes; and periwinkle as a tea to treat coughs and diabetes.

ORCHIDS: The **wild banana orchid** is the national flower, selected from among 27 indigenous orchid species. Blooming in April and May, this orchid is found on all three islands, but in different varieties. On Grand Cayman, look for *Schomburgkia thomsoniana*, with one-inch white blossoms and purple lips. On Cayman Brac and Little Cayman, the *Shomburgkia thomsoniana var. minor* is yellow in color with lighter purple lips. In all, 26 species of orchids are found on the islands, with five not found anywhere else. (Don't plan on viewing all the varieties, however; some are so small you'd need a magnifying glass to spot them!)

HURRICANE CATEGORIES

Atlantic hurricanes are ranked by the Saffir-Simpson intensity scale to give an estimate of the potential flooding and damage. Category Three and above are considered intense.

Category/Winds (mph)	Damage
One/74 - 95	*Minimal:* Damage primarily to shrubbery, trees and foliage.
Two/96 - 110	*Moderate:* Considerable damage to shrubbery and foliage; some trees blown down. Some damage to roofing materials.
Three/111 - 130	*Extensive:* Foliage torn from trees; large trees down. Some structural damage to small buildings. Mobile homes destroyed. Coastal flooding.
Four/131 - 155	*Extreme:* Shrubs and trees blown down. Complete failure of roofs on small residences. Major beach erosion. Massive evacuation of all homes within 500 yards of shore possibly required. Hurricane Andrew that smashed into S. Florida in 1992 is a good example of a "force four."
Five/155+	*Catastrophic:* Some complete building failures. Small buildings overturned/blown away. Low-lying escape routes inland cut by rising water three-five hours before the hurricane's center arrives. Hurricane Camille, category five, struck Mississippi and Louisiana in 1969.

Introduction

TREES: The national tree is the **silver thatch palm** (*Coccothrinax proctoril*). Named for botanist Dr. George Proctor, author of *Flora of the Cayman Islands* (see *Booklist*), the palm has a silvery underside with light green upper fronds. For all its beauty, this plant has far more than ornamental value, though. It has been used by islanders to form roofing, belts, baskets, rope, and more. Palm rope has long been a bartering tool, traded for staples.

The **mango** is the most plentiful fruit in the Cayman Islands, ripening in the month of June and continuing to produce fruit through September. The islands harvest about 65,000 pounds of this tropical treasure every season. There are 15 different varieties of the fruit; you'll find it at roadside stands and farmers' markets.

Animals

A shy resident of these islands is the **agouti** (*Dasyprocta punctata*), a rabbit-sized rodent once hunted for meat. The agouti is a Central American native, introduced by the early settlers. Once kept as a pet and raised for food, today the rodent is rarely seen. The agouti has long, thin legs, hoof-like claws with three toes on its hind feet and five toes on its forefeet. A family of agoutis can be viewed at the Cayman Turtle Farm on Grand Cayman.

The **hickatee** (*Trachemys decussata*), a freshwater turtle, is found in the freshwater and brackish ponds in the Cayman Islands and neighboring Cuba.

Although the Cayman Islands have no poisonous snakes, you might spot a harmless indigenous species, such as the **grass snake** (*Alsophis cantherigerus*). The numbers of this snake, which feeds on frogs and lizards, have been reduced by the mongoose, which was introduced to the islands to control rats. (Unfortunately, rats and mongooses keep different hours, so the mongoose feeds on snakes instead. As snakes are a natural predator of rats, the rat population is burgeoning now.)

A favorite sighting is the **blue iguana** (*cyclura nubila lewisi*). This vegetarian species can grow to a length of five feet. It's often seen sunning (sometimes in the middle of the road). Little Cayman is home to over 2,000 iguanas (check out the "iguana crossing" signs around the island). On Grand Cayman, you can see a large male in the Queen Elizabeth II Botanic Gardens.

The majestic blue iguana.

Bird Life

Bird life thrives. Parrots, ducks, cuckoos, herons, and others populate the wetlands. Birders are challenged by numerous species on all three islands.

One of the most exotic species is the Cayman national bird, the **Cayman parrot.** You might hear this bird even before you see its iridescent green feathers. Look for the birds in early morning and late afternoon when they return to roost in the stumps of palm trees. On Grand Cayman, look for the **Grand Cayman parrot** (*Amazona leucocephala caymensis*); Cayman Brac boasts a subspecies, the **Cayman Brac parrot** (*Amazona leucocephala hesterna*), one of the world's rarest Amazon parrots. (Don't scan the trees looking for parrots on Little Cayman. The island's parrots disappeared in 1932 with the Great Hurricane and never returned.) These parrots eat fruit, flowers and seeds in the dry woodlands and nest in hollow trees.

Introduction

Another common bird is the **Zenaida dove** (*zenaida aurita*), a cooing dove that hunts for dried seeds. The colorful **bananaquit**, a yellow and black bird that's not shy about begging for crumbs (and its favorite treat: sugar) is another common sight. Although bananaquits are found throughout the Caribbean, the bananaquit (*coereba flaveola sharpei*) found in the Cayman Islands is a unique subspecies.

Red-footed boobies (*sula sula*) are easily sighted on Little Cayman. Here you'll find 7,000 boobies, about 30% of the Caribbean population. This beige bird, about 25 inches in size, nests high in the trees, constructing a rough nest of sticks that's easy to spot. Its young are pure white.

Magnificent frigate birds are also sighted in these islands. With a wingspan of over seven feet and wings sharply angled like boomerangs, the black frigate bird is fairly easy to spot. They soar high over the sea and are aggressive to other birds, often hitting the red-footed booby in flight in an attempt to make it disgorge its meal, an easy dinner for the frigate bird.

Little Cayman in particular is a favorite with birders, who come to the tiny isle for the chance to spot red-footed boobies, magnificent frigate birds, West Indian whistling ducks, cattle egrets, black necked stilts, snowy egrets, tricolored herons, and others. Cayman Brac is favored for its parrot viewing, with a large reserve dedicated to these colorful birds. Grand Cayman is also home to several protected areas and ponds where both migrating and resident birds thrive.

Much of the credit for the proliferation and recognition of the Cayman Islands' bird life can be taken by former Governor Michael Gore. An avid birder, Gore worked diligently to secure the many sites and preserve them for future enjoyment.

 EARTH WATCH: *Capturing of Cayman parrots is illegal. Formerly a popular house pet on the islands, both subspecies are now protected by law and cannot be taken from the wild.*

Marine Life

The marine life here is some of the richest in the Caribbean. Gargonians, barrel and tube sponges, and other colorful formations make the experience extraordinary for even the most seasoned divers.

Stingrays

There's no doubt that for many travelers the Cayman Islands are synonymous with stingrays, thanks to the popularity of Stingray City. These fascinating creatures are most commonly seen in the area of the North Sound where the bay spills into the sea, but are sometimes sighted in other places as well. Many types of rays frequent this part of the Caribbean:

◆ **Southern Atlantic stingray** (*dasyatis americana*). This is the most common type of stingray and these are the fellows that will come up and nuzzle up to your hand at Stingray City and the Sandbar on the North Sound. They're found in shallow bays near the sandy bottoms where they feed on mollusks and crustaceans. Considered a choice meal by sharks, the rays have a barbed tail for protection. Like a scorpion's tail, the barb is brought up to defend the ray against attack from above. These rays are either a dark gray or brown with a white belly. They can reach up to six feet in width.

◆ **Eagle rays** are spotted along the walls (most often along the North Wall of Grand Cayman) and are wary of people. Like the stingrays, eagles are also white-bellied but have patterned topsides, with spots and circles in a white or beige color against a dark gray or brown. These rays have angular pectoral fins and can measure up to eight feet across.

◆ **Manta rays.** These are the largest of the ray family, growing over 20 feet across and sometimes weighing in at over 3,000 pounds. They have a unique fin structure around their mouths that forms a scoop to gulp plankton and small organisms. An immature manta was spotted for several years off Little Cayman but has not been sighted recently.

Introduction

Sea Turtles

Other marine life often associated with the Cayman Islands are sea turtles. There's no missing the importance of this marine creature in the Cayman Islands. Sir Turtle, the islands' peg-legged turtle "mascot," is seen on every brochure you'll find, and the most popular land attraction on this island is the Cayman Turtle Farm.

A visit to the Cayman Turtle Farm.

The **green sea turtle** (*chelonia mydas*) that is such an integral part of Cayman culture is found in the Atlantic, Gulf of Mexico, Mediterranean, Pacific and Indian Oceans. These turtles have been observed to remain underwater for several days without surfacing for air. Even in their current protected state, the turtle does not lead an easy life; only one out of 10,000 eggs laid reaches maturity. The hazards are many: birds, animals, marine life, humans. Everything's a threat to these little guys. Nevertheless, the turtle thrives in Cayman waters.

EARTH WATCH: *The Cayman Islands have taken strict measures to protect marine life. Today, the sea turtle is protected and no one may disturb, molest, or take turtles in Cayman waters without a license. Other marine conservation laws prohibit the taking of any marine life or damaging coral with anchors. Over 200 permanent boat moorings are in place around the islands.*

MARINE CONSERVATION LAWS

The Cayman Islands have some of the strictest marine conservation laws in place in the Caribbean. The laws were first put into place in 1978 and were strengthened in 1993. The rules prohibit: damaging coral by anchor, chains or any other means anywhere in Cayman waters; the taking of any marine life while scuba diving; the taking of any coral, sponges, sea fans or other marine specimens; the use of a spear gun or seine net; fishing with gill nets or poison; dumping anything into the water; exporting any form of marine life.

Basically, the law designates four special areas for protection: marine park zones, replenishment zones, environmental zones, and no-diving zones.

In **marine park zones** it is illegal to take any marine life, alive or dead, except by line fishing from the shore or beyond the drop-off. Anchoring is permitted only at fixed moorings installed by the Department of Environment's Protection and Conservation unit.

Lobster and conch are protected in the **replenishment zones**. Spear guns, pole spears, fish traps, and fish nets are also prohibited in these regions; only line fishing is allowed. Anchoring is permitted.

Environmental zones receive some of the strictest protection under the law. Here, no marine life may be taken or disturbed; anchoring is prohibited, as are all activities in the water. Part of the North Sound on Grand Cayman is covered by these stringent rules in order to protect breeding areas for fish and other marine life.

No-diving zones were created to protect the cultural heritage as well as the environment of the Cayman Islands. This designation marks a region as off-limits for scuba diving to protect the waters for traditional Cayman fishing. These special zones have been set aside off the north coast of Grand Cayman.

Marine law also limits the amount of catch. Lobster can be caught only during season (closed season: February 1 through July 31). During season, only adult spiny lobster with a six-inch minimum tail size may be taken. Each person may take up to five or no more than 15 per boat per day. Up to 15 conch may be taken per person (or 20 per boat). Only adult conchs, those with fully developed lips, may be harvested. Grouper are protected during the winter spawning season (January).

The penalty for violation of any of these marine rules is strict. The maximum penalty is CI $5,000 (US $6,000) and one year in jail. The penalty for vessels convicted of illegally dumping waste is CI $500,000 (US $625,000).

For more about the Marine Conservation Laws, ask for a copy of the brochure *Marine Park Rules and The Sea Code in the Cayman Islands*; or call the Cayman Islands Dept. of Environment's Protection and Conservation Unit on Grand Cayman at ☎ (345) 949-8469 or fax (345) 949-8912.

Environmental Organizations

Several organizations welcome visitors to their regular meetings to learn more about the environment and culture of the island. Check out one of these groups during your next visit:

National Trust for the Cayman Islands
P.O. Box 31116 SMB
Grand Cayman, Cayman Islands, BWI
☎ (345) 949-0121, fax (345) 949-7494
E-mail: ntrust@candw.ky

Cayman Islands National Archive
Grand Cayman, Cayman Islands, BWI
☎ (345) 949-9345, fax (345) 949-9727

CAYFEST, National Festival of the Arts
P.O. Box 30301 SMB
Grand Cayman, Cayman Islands, BWI
☎ (345) 949-5839

Queen Elizabeth II Botanic Park
Andrew Guthrie, Manager
P.O. Box 30865 SMB
Grand Cayman, Cayman Islands, BWI
☎ (345) 947-9469, fax (345) 947-7873
E-mail: guthrie@candw.ky

Cayman Islands Bird Club
c/o National Trust
P.O. Box 31116 SMB
Grand Cayman, Cayman Islands, BWI
☎ (345) 949-0121, fax (345) 949-7494
E-mail: ntrust@candw.ky
Meetings are held on the last Tuesday of every
month, 7:15 p.m., at the offices at the National
Trust. Informal meetings are held most Saturday
mornings; October is a very active month.

Garden Club of Grand Cayman
P.O. Box 30447 SMB
Grand Cayman, Cayman Islands, BWI
☎ (800) 949-7965, (345) 945-1709
Monthly meetings; annual flower show in May.

Grand Cayman Orchid Society
P.O. Box 30083 SMB
Grand Cayman, Cayman Islands, BWI
☎ (345) 949-5564
Monthly meetings.

Government/Economy

The Cayman Islands are a dependent territory, or a British Crown
Colony, of the United Kingdom. The islands are led by the

Governor, an appointee of the Queen. The Governor leads the Executive Council, which includes three official and four elected members. The unicameral legislature consists of 15 members. The government offices are found on Elgin Street in George Town, the capital of the Cayman Islands. Grand Cayman is divided into districts: Bodden Town, East End, George Town, North Side, Savannah, and West Bay.

Throughout the Cayman Islands, you'll see the official flag flying: a red banner with a small union jack in the upper left corner. The outside half of the flag includes a Caymanian coat of arms with a pineapple and turtle above a shield with three stars to symbolize the three islands. Across the bottom reads the motto of the Cayman Islands: He Hath Founded it Upon the Seas.

The economy of the Cayman Islands is one of the strongest in the Caribbean and residents enjoy one of the highest standards of living in the world. The average household income is CI $56,000 (US $68,292), with a low unemployment rate. Much of that affluence results from the successful tourism industry, with about 70% of the national product coming from that sector. Last year over $250 million was added to local coffers because of tourism. The popularity of the islands continues to rise, and the most recent figures show 1,144,313 visitors. Just over 373,000 arrive by air and 771,000 by cruise ship. Those figures are up by 100,000 from the previous year. Most visitors come from the United States. During the winter season, many vacationers arrive from the East and Midwest; in hot summer months a great number from Texas and the South make their way to these islands for their cooler temperatures.

Offshore financial services play an integral role. Grand Cayman has nearly 600 licensed banks (including 47 branches representing the 50 largest banks worldwide). Banking secrecy laws passed in 1966 laid the groundwork for this profitable industry that today puts the small island in the same league as financial giants such as Zurich and Tokyo. Just what is a Cayman banking account? Some are, as might be expected, multi-million dollar accounts, while others are on a much smaller scale. Both take advantage of the tax-free status and confidentiality laws, which protect all reputable transactions as a means for earning tax-free interest. You can open an account once the Caymanian bank receives a reference from your home banker, then you can deposit funds (in US dollars, if you like). There is no exchange control and money can be moved in and out of the country freely and privately. Banks normally don't accept huge amounts of cash.

Offshore insurance companies are also a growing business. Nearly 400 offshore insurance or captive insurance companies make their base here. (Captive insurance is a term used for insurance companies set up by a company or a trade association to serve its members or employees.) Thanks to Cayman Islands' generous tax-free status, many other companies choose to incorporate in the islands; currently almost 30,000 companies are registered there.

NATIONAL SYMBOLS

Unofficial national symbol:	Sir Turtle, a peg-legged swashbuckling turtle
National bird:	Cayman parrot
National tree:	Silver thatch palm
National flower:	Wild banana orchid

Sir Turtle welcomes you to Grand Cayman.

People/Culture

The three Cayman Islands boast a total population just over 33,000. About 32,000 people reside on the largest island, followed by 1,200 residents on Cayman Brac and a scant 120 on Little Cayman.

It's a varied population, with cultures from around the globe. About a third of all residents are non-Caymanians. Most are from the US, Canada, the UK and nearby Jamaica, although a total of 113 nationalities are represented.

English is the primary language in the Cayman Islands, but you'll notice it is spoken with a unique lilt, one a little different from accents in other areas of the Caribbean. It's a reminder of the islands' earliest Welsh, Scottish, and English settlers. You'll often hear the Jamaican patois as well.

EARTH WATCH: *The islands are home to the* ***Cayman Islands Humane Society****, a non-profit organization that offers low-cost neutering and spaying programs and finds homes for stray pets. For more information,* ☎ *(345) 945-2668. Donations can be sent to the Cayman Islands Humane Society, P.O. Box 1167, George Town, Grand Cayman, BWI.*

Caymanian cuisine reflects the riches of the sea. Traditional Caymanian food includes turtle, brought to the table in the form of soup, stew, or steak, and conch (pronounced konk), the mollusc that lives in the beautiful pink-and-white shell seen throughout the islands. Conch is a versatile dish and may be served as an appetizer in the form of fritters, a soup prepared as a chowder or thick with onions and spices as a stew, or even uncooked, marinated in lime juice as ceviche.

The influences of nearby Jamaica are seen on island menus as well, especially in the jerk seasoning that ignites fish, chicken, and other meats. Jerk is meat or fish slathered with a fiery concoction of scotch bonnet peppers, allspice, thyme, salt, garlic, scallions, and onions, then slow-cooked over a flame to produce a dish similar to a piquant barbecue. As in Jamaica, jerk is often served with rice and beans (usually pigeon peas), a traditional Caribbean side dish.

Other Caribbean favorites found in the Cayman Islands include breadfruit (similar in taste to a potato, and served in as many ways), cassava (another potato-like vegetable), fish tea (a broth-like soup), johnny cake (fried bread), patty (a meat pie that's a Caribbean standard as popular as the American hamburger), pumpkin soup (using Caribbean pumpkins, which are not sweet), saltfish (dried and salted codfish), and ackee (a fruit that tastes somewhat like scrambled eggs and, for breakfast, is served with saltfish).

With residents and visitors from around the world, however, the Cayman Islands also offer many other types of cuisine, especially on Grand Cayman.

Using This Book

This book is divided into four parts. The introductory section you have just read looks at the geography, history, flora and fauna of the islands. The next section covers Customs and Immigration and also gives details that will help you get around the islands, whether that means jumping in an open-air jeep or an eight-seater island-hopping plane. This section also includes an overview of the types of adventures available in the Cayman Islands.

GRAND CAYMAN: The second section covers the island of Grand Cayman, the heart of Caymanian tourism and the destination for most travelers. For easy navigation, we have divided the island into four regions.

◆ **East of George Town** takes a look at the land, much of it unimproved swamp and buttonwood forest, stretching east of the capital city of George Town. A favorite of birders, hikers, and those seeking a look at the flora and fauna of the islands, the East End is little changed from its days before the boom in Cayman tourism. This is the quietest part of Grand Cayman and well worth a day trip even for those staying on other areas of the island.

◆ **George Town** covers the capital city, the heart of the business and banking industry that has made these islands so affluent. The stop of all cruise ship passengers, George Town is also the best place for those looking to learn more about Caymanian history, to do some duty-free shopping, and to enjoy some of the island's best underwater fun.

◆ The **Seven Mile Beach** section explores what for many travelers *is* the Cayman Islands, a stretch of powdery beach lined not just with palms and casuarina trees, but also with resorts, condominiums, and innumerable watersports operators. The heart of the Caymanian tourism business, this is one of the most popular beaches in the Caribbean.

◆ **West Bay** takes a look at the region to the north of Seven Mile Beach, a quiet residential section that's also home to some of the island's top tourism attractions: the Turtle Farm and Hell.

CAYMAN BRAC: The third chapter covers the largest of the Sister Islands: Cayman Brac. A favorite of scuba divers, this island boasts a neighborly feeling, a sense of peacefulness, and a striking landscape.

LITTLE CAYMAN: The last section takes a look at the tiniest treasure in the Cayman Islands: Little Cayman. A favorite with birders and anglers, this 10-square-mile island is a giant in the scuba diving world and home of Bloody Bay Wall, named by Philippe Cousteau as one of the best dive sites in the world. Although a veritable metropolis below the surface, with high-rise coral heads and a marine population explosion, on land all's quiet and secluded. Only a handful of permanent residents are lucky enough to make their home on this limestone isle that offers quiet inns and a few condominiums.

Adventures

Each of the chapters includes adventures to be had in its particular region. "Adventure" is a term for you to define based on your own interests, limitations, and abilities. Throughout this book we offer a variety of sporting and eco-tourism options both on and off land. Whether adventure travel means wreck diving or birdwatching, you'll find it covered in these sections, but keep in mind that you should set you own boundaries here.

Regardless of the type of activity you choose, know your limits. Scuba adventures in these islands range from beginners' dives in shallow, placid waters to deep wall and wreck dives. Hikes vary from strolls to sweaty workouts. On the water fun spans the spectrum as well, with some vacationers wrestling a fighting bonefish or marlin while others skip across the sea atop a waverunner or breeze along in a catamaran.

At all times, it is important to maintain your fluid levels. At this latitude, temperatures (and humidity levels) soar, draining away precious water and minerals from your body. Replenish them often, and be sure to carry water on all hikes and boating excursions.

Sun, while being one of the islands' biggest draws, is also a factor to be closely monitored. Wear a hat and a good sunscreen at all times (SPF 15 or higher).

Where to Stay

Each chapter also gives you nuts-and-bolts information on transportation, attractions, accommodations, and dining. Unless noted otherwise, pricing is given in US dollars, commonly used on all the islands.

We've sought to give a variety of price ranges in both accommodations and dining. Note, however, that rates change quickly, so use these as a gauge and not a figure set in stone. Accommodation rates are given in the listings for high season, but keep in mind that these vary greatly by season, soaring to the highest limits from mid-December through mid-April (and hitting a real peak the week between Christmas and New Year's) then dropping to a low during summer and fall months. Contact the hotels directly for the best prices and possible package deals that may save you money.

Accommodation prices are given with dollar signs to indicate the price for a standard room for one night during high season (expect prices to be as much as 40% lower during the low season). Prices are given in US dollars.

$	under $150
$$	between $150 and $300
$$$	over $300

Where to Eat

We've also covered an array of dining opportunities in these chapters, from fast food burgers to haute cuisine that will set you back the cost of a day's vacation.

Restaurant prices are given with dollar signs that indicate the price of a meal, drink, and gratuity, according to the following scales:

$	under $15 per person
$$	$15 to $30 per person
$$$	$30 to $45 per person

Travel Information, When To Go

Regardless of when you visit, you're almost always assured of short-sleeve weather, balmy tradewinds, and plenty of sun. Temperatures vary about 10° between summer and winter. The hottest months are July and August, when average temperatures top out at 85 to 90°. The coolest month is February, when highs range from 72 to 86° and nighttime lows dip to the mid-60s to lower 70s.

Water temperatures drop slightly during the winter months, when they range from 78 to 82°. During the summer, the waters warm to about 85°, a balmy bath-like temperature that makes wetsuits strictly optional.

For a current weather report, call the **Cayman Islands National Meteorological Service** in George Town at ☎ (345) 945-5773 or check the weather page on the Cayman Islands Web site (http://www.caymans.com).

Immigration & Customs

United States and Canadian citizens need to show proof of citizenship in the form of a passport or birth certificate. Visitors must also show a return airline ticket.

Travelers can remain in the islands for up to six months. To extend your visit you must obtain permission by writing the Chief Immigration Officer, Department of Immigration, P.O. Box 1098, Grand Cayman. On island, the immigration offices are found at the Government Admin. Building on Elgin Avenue in George Town.

Visitors are allowed to bring in duty-free one liter of alcohol, four liters of wine or one case of beer, and 200 cigarettes, 50 cigars or 250 grams of tobacco.

Upon leaving the Cayman Islands, there is a departure tax of US $12.50 for every person 12 years or older. (This is not payable by credit card.) This has been raised from the former $10 per person to include a new $2.50 environmental protection fee. There is no departure tax for inter-island travel within the Cayman Islands.

The Cayman Islands are a duty-free port, so after 48 hours out of the States, Americans can return home with up to US $400 in purchases without paying duty. (Families may pool their exemptions; a husband and wife can take an exemption of $800, a family of four $1,600.) Cayman crafts are exempt from this allowance, as are works of art, foreign language books, caviar, and truffles.

Turtle products – shells, steaks, lotion, and shell jewelry – sold on the island cannot be brought back into the US or through the US in transit to other countries. Skip these items at the Cayman Turtle Farm gift shop.

Each visitor can also return with one carton of cigarettes and two liters of alcohol (only visitors age 21 and over). Additional liquor purchases result in a duty approximately 15% above the duty-free cost.

Travel Information

UNITED STATES CUSTOMS

When you leave the US, then return home, you will pass through US Customs at your point of US entry. (A few islands have Customs Pre-Clearance so you can go through the declaration before returning home, usually a faster process.)

You'll complete a Customs declaration form, one per household, identifying the total amount of your expenditures while out of the country. Each returning Cayman visitor has an exemption of $400.

Your duty-free allowance includes any items purchased in duty-free shops, gifts presented to you, gifts you bought in the islands for other people, and purchases you might be wearing, such as clothing or jewelry.

The US Department of Agriculture allows you to bring back up to one ounce of decorative beach sand. Some items cannot be brought back to the US. These include:

◆ books or cassettes made without authorized copyright ("pirated" copies)

◆ any type of drug paraphernalia

◆ firearms

◆ fruits, vegetables and meats/meat by-products (such as pâté)

◆ plants, cuttings

◆ tortoiseshell jewelry or other turtle products (which are sold in the Cayman Islands)

To make your passage through Customs a little easier, you should keep your sales slips and pack so your purchases can be easily reached. Get a copy of the *Know Before You Go* brochure (Publication 512) from the US Customs Service at your airport or by writing the US Customs Service, P.O. Box 7407, Washington, DC 20044.

Cost

Cayman is costly, there's no denying it. The Cayman dollar is stronger than its US equivalent, exchanged at a rate of US $1.25 to CI $1. Prices in hotels, restaurants, stores, and attractions reflect that unfavorable exchange rate and the high standard of living enjoyed on the island. Just how expensive is it? Accommodation prices vary with the season. High season, spanning from mid-December to mid-April, is the most expensive time to plan a visit. Rates are at their peak during this time and during the Christmas holidays expect prices to soar even higher. The least expensive time to visit is during the summer months when prices may be as much as 40% lower. To many visitors, the best combination of price and weather comes during the "shoulder seasons," the months sandwiched before and after high season. Prices are lower, the seas are usually calm, and the livin' is easy.

Although room prices fluctuate with the season, food and transportation costs remain stable. Food, of course, varies with the type of restaurant, but expect to pay about 30% more than you'd pay at home for a comparable meal. Even fast food establishments offer standard favorites with a price tag a little heftier than you are accustomed to seeing. Even while trying to cut costs, we've paid US $50 for burgers and soft drinks for three at seaside lunch spots. To combat high prices, many repeat Cayman visitors prefer to prepare a meal or two a day "at home." Condominium units with full housekeeping facilities are exceedingly popular, especially on Grand Cayman. Some vacationers even go as far as bringing along ice chests packed with staples. Here are a few money-saving tips in the Cayman Islands:

- ◆ Consider bringing some food with you or making a stop at a supermarket in George Town.

- ◆ Pick up coupon booklets at the airport. These can include 10%-off coupons and other bargains at eateries on Grand Cayman.

- ◆ Look for two-for-one specials (popular on Sunday nights).

- ◆ Buy rum on-island and make your own drinks.

◆ Double-check the gratuity. Some restaurants add a 15% gratuity to the bill, so make sure you don't inadvertently tip twice.

◆ Check for laundry facilities if you rent a condominium.

◆ Look for early bird specials at some restaurants. Dining before 6 p.m. can save money.

◆ Make sure you understand whether the menu prices you are reading are marked in US or CI dollars.

PRICE CHART
(Prices in CI dollars)

Coke	$0.80
12-pack of soft drinks	$4.30
Bar of soap	$1.00
Bag of chips	$3.00
Gallon (imperial) of gas	$2.28

(Gas is sold by the US gallon on Little Cayman and runs about $2.38.)

You'll find that grocery prices are slightly higher on Little Cayman and Cayman Brac because all items must be brought in from the larger island.

Holidays

Festivals

Throughout the calendar year, Cayman Islanders celebrate with special events. You'll find activities aimed at fishermen, preservationists, pilots, scuba divers, and those who just want to have a good time.

PIRATES WEEK: The biggest blowout of the year is Pirates Week, scheduled annually at the end of October. It's a shiver-me-timbers time when the islands celebrate their buccaneering history with treasure hunts, parades, and plenty of excuses to dress as pirates and wenches. The celebration begins with fireworks and continues with parades, a 5K run, an underwater treasure hunt, a golf tournament, triathlon, sailboard race, children's fun fair, and much more.

Although swashbuckling may be the theme of Pirates Week, Caymanian heritage is also emphasized during this festival. Reenactments of an old time Caymanian wedding, thatch craft, and more have entertained and educated visitors at past festivals. Local foods, such as stewed conch, fish tea, and coconut rundown, are served, and traditional quadrille dancing is highlighted.

MILLION DOLLAR MONTH: The month of June is Million Dollar Month, when fishermen from far and near come to try their luck. Residents as well as visitors from around the world enter this tournament. The grand prize is US $250,000, awarded to the first angler to break the existing Cayman Islands All-Tackle Record for Atlantic blue marlin. The current record of 584 pounds was set in 1984. Other prizes include US $250,000 to the boat landing the largest blue marlin over 300 pounds; US $50,000 each to the boats landing the heaviest dolphin, wahoo, and yellowfin tuna; and US $50,000 to the boat of a single angler landing the largest Grand Slam (heaviest combined weight of a dolphin, wahoo, and yellowfin tuna). The visiting angler who reels in the largest eligible fish is awarded US $5,000.

The tournament begins at The Links at SafeHaven. Registration is US $200 (plus boat charter expenses) and is open to amateur and professional anglers. Boat/group registration fees are US $1,000.

This tournament draws over 200 anglers. Conservation rules apply, and fishermen are encouraged to release any catches under 300 pounds. Only those fish caught in sanctioned Million Dollar Month boats are eligible for the cash boat prizes and registered anglers can fish only on the Queen's Birthday (June 16), the day of the Mermaids Tournament, and weekends (Friday through Sunday). For more information, contact **MDM Headquarters**, P.O. Box 878 George Town, Grand Cayman, ☎ (345) 949-5587, fax (345) 949-5528.

AVIATION WEEK: Another peak time is International Aviation Week in early June. Sponsored by the Cayman Islands Department of Tourism, Aviation Week features an air show over Seven Mile

Travel Information

Beach, displays, safety seminars, and live air-sea rescue demonstrations. Private pilots from throughout the states (including many who might not be comfortable making the journey alone) travel in a caravan from Key West, Florida, across Cuba's Giron corridor on the 330-nautical-mile route. In recent years, this "invasion" has included over 150 private planes.

Public Holidays

During public holidays, expect all government offices and most retail establishments to close.

January 1	New Year's Day
February	Ash Wednesday
March	Good Friday, Easter Monday
May 19	Discovery Day
June 16	Queen's Birthday
July (first Monday)	Constitution Day
November 10	Remembrance Day
December 25	Christmas Day
December 26	Boxing Day

Cultural Festivities

If you're interested in learning more about the culture of the Cayman Islands, an excellent time to visit is during Cayfest. Scheduled for several weeks in July, Cayfest is a national festival of the arts of the Cayman Islands. It includes theater, dance, painting, pottery, architecture, photography, and more. Check out traditional Caymanian arts and dances, such as the quadrille. For more information, contact the **Cayman National Cultural Foundation** at ☎ (345) 949-5839.

CALENDAR

You'll find plenty of rollicking festivals throughout the year. Here's a sampling of some which are planned annually:

January
   Windsurfing Regatta at Cayman Windsurf,
      Morritt's Tortuga Club.

February
   Mardi Gras Parade, Little Cayman.
   Cayman Islands Angling Club Annual Wahoo
      Tournament.
   National Children's Festival of Arts.

March
   St. Patrick's Day Jog, Hyatt Britannia Golf Course.
   Boat Show, Grand Cayman Sailing Club.
   Easter Regatta, Round the Islands Sailing Race.
   Easter Bash, Little Cayman (fundraiser for the
      Little Cayman District Committee of the National
      Trust).
   Humane Society Dog Show.

April
   Earth Day Celebration.
   Tuna Tournament, Cayman Islands Angling Club.
   Rotary BATABANO Carnival.

May
   "Responsible Diver" Month.
   Garden Club Flower Show, Treasure Island Resort.
   "Shoot-Out" Fishing Tournament, C.I. Angling
      Club.

June
   Million Dollar Month International Fishing
      Tournament.
   Cayman Islands International Aviation Week.

July
   Taste of Cayman.
   Chili Cook-Off.
   Culinary Competition and Presentation of
      Culinary Awards of Excellence.
   Kiwanis Golf Tournament.

Travel Information

August
> One Day Light Tackle Shoot Out, Cayman Angling
>   Club.
> Cayman Madness Dive Vacation Promotion.
> National Trust for the Cayman Island's Annual
>   Trust Fair.

September
> Cayfest National Arts Festival.
> Cayman Madness.
> Rotary International Fishing Tournament.

October
> Pirates Week.
> National Trust Haunted House Fundraiser.

November
> Tackle Fishing Tournament, Cayman Islands
>   Angling Club.
> Cayman Islands Angling Club All Tackle
>   Tournament.
> Birthday Celebration, National Museum.

December
> Christmas House Lighting Competition.
> Arrival of Santa Claus, Owens Roberts
> International
>   Airport.
> Rotary Christmas Tree Lighting and Carols,
>   George Town.

Transportation

Air Service

You'll arrive in the Cayman Islands at Owen Roberts International Airport, a stylish facility that resembles a Polynesian structure. The principle carrier into this port of entry is **Cayman Airways** (☎ 800-G-CAYMAN), the national carrier with flights from Miami, Tampa, Orlando, and Houston. Flights to Grand Cayman from Miami average about 70 minutes.

Service is also available with American Airlines from Miami (and Raleigh-Durham during high season), Northwest Airlines from Miami and Detroit, USAirways International from Charlotte and Tampa, and America Trans Air from Indianapolis, Seattle and Chicago. Additional carriers include Air Jamaica, Canadian, Sunworld, Taesa, Royal, Sun Country, Cubana, and British Airways with twice-weekly service from London.

AIR SERVICE TO THE CAYMAN ISLANDS

Air Jamaica	☎ (800) 523-5585
American	☎ (800) 433-7300
Cayman Airways	☎ (800) 422-9626
from Canada	☎ (800) 441-3003
Island Air	☎ (800) 922-9626
	or (345) 949-0241
Northwest	☎ (800) 225-2525
USAirways	☎ (800) 622-1015
United	☎ (800) 241-6522

Direct flights to Cayman Brac are available from Miami, Tampa, Atlanta, and Houston or from Grand Cayman. Service to Little Cayman is available only with Island Air from Grand Cayman or Cayman Brac. Departure tax is US $12.50 per person; no tax charged for inter-island travel.

Island Hopping

Island hopping is part of life in the Cayman Islands; both Little Cayman and Cayman Brac are served by small aircraft rather than ferries. Cayman Air offers twice daily service to Cayman Brac from Grand Cayman, except on Tuesday and Wednesday. **Island Air** (☎ 345-949-5252, Monday through Friday, 9 a.m. to 5 p.m.; fax 345-949-7044) provides daily service between the three islands.

The flight from Grand Cayman to Little Cayman takes 45 minutes; the aircraft continues on to Cayman Brac after a short stop. Passengers may check up to 55 pounds of baggage free of charge; excess baggage is charged US 50¢ per pound.

Fares from Grand Cayman to Little Cayman or Cayman Brac are US $122 round-trip or US $105 for the day trip (there and back in one day). Flights between Cayman Brac and Little Cayman are US $40 round-trip. Special fares are available for children under 12.

INTER-ISLAND FLIGHT SCHEDULE

Flight times and prices are subject to change; call Island Air for bookings and times.

Grand Cayman to Little Cayman
Departs 8 a.m. & 3:50 p.m.; arrives 8:45 a.m. & 4:35 p.m.

Little Cayman to Grand Cayman
Departs 9:55 a.m. & 5:45 p.m.; arrives 10:40 a.m. & 6:30 p.m.

Grand Cayman to Cayman Brac
Departs 8:00 a.m. & 3:50 p.m.; arrives 9:10 a.m. & 5 p.m.

Cayman Brac to Grand Cayman
Departs 9:30 a.m. & 5:20 p.m.; arrives 10:40 a.m. & 6:30 p.m.

Cayman Brac to Little Cayman
Departs 9:30 a.m. & 5:20 p.m.; arrives 9:45 a.m. & 5:25 p.m.

Little Cayman to Cayman Brac
Departs 8:55 a.m. & 4:45 p.m.; arrives 9:10 a.m. & 5 p.m.

Cruise Service

Grand Cayman limits the number of cruise ships that can be in port at any time to three or four, with a maximum capacity of 5,500 passengers. This limit ensures that everyone has a good experience while on the island and nobody feels overcrowded in George Town.

Grand Cayman is served by numerous cruise lines, including Norwegian, Princess, Regal, Royal Caribbean, Royal, Sun Line, Carnival, Celebrity, Costa, Crystal, Crown Commodore, Cunard, Dolphin, Holland America, and others.

EARTH WATCH: *Grand Cayman is just completing the first of three permanent cruise ship moorings in the George Town Harbour. Designed to protect the fragile coral reefs from anchor damage, this $184,000 project has been contracted to the Tampa-based marine engineering firm of Moffat and Nichol. An ongoing 10-month geo-technical study has determinined the kind of moorings required and their optimal locations, and will continue to measure the environmental impact of the project.*

Cruise ship passengers arrive by tender in George Town at either the North or South Terminal (just steps apart). Both terminals are right in the heart of George Town, just a stroll from shopping and dining. The clean waterfront brims with shops featuring fine jewelry, black coral, artwork, leather goods, and more.

Visitors arriving for the day will find plenty of drivers offering trips to Seven Mile Beach as well as island tours just steps from the cruise terminals. You'll find a selection of organized tours (typically to the Turtle Farm, Hell, and Seven Mile Beach) for about $25 (a two-hour tour around the island). See *Guided Tours*, below. To experience the island without the crowds, consider hiring a driver by the hour. A taxi stand is located at the terminal and a knowledgeable driver will take up to four persons for US $37.50 per hour.

If you'd rather spend your time on the beach, take a taxi directly to Seven Mile Beach, about three miles from town. Taxi fare runs about US $4 per person each way; a steady flow of taxis from the hotels to town insures that you'll have no difficulty returning to town.

Generally, the busiest cruise ship days are Tuesday, Wednesday, and Thursday. If you're not onboard a ship and want to visit George Town during a quiet day, plan to shop on Monday or Friday. (Not all shops are open on Saturdays, and many close on Sundays.)

Travel Information

PACKAGE TOUR OPERATORS

Contact these outfits to see what they have on offer:

AA Fly-Away Vacations	☎ (800) 321-2121
Cayman Airtours	☎ (800) 247-2966
Cayman Airways Holidays	☎ (800) G-CAYMAN
Delta's Dream Vacations	☎ (800) 872-7786

General tour packages:
Caribbean Concepts
575 Underhill Boulevard, Syosset, NY 11791
☎ (800) 423-4433

Horizon Tours
1634 I St., NW, Suite 301, Washington, DC 20006
☎ (800) 395-0025

Liberty Travel
101 2nd St. West, Chaska, MN 55318
☎ (800) 216-9776

Adventure and environmental tours:
National Audubon Society
700 Broadway, New York, NY 10003
☎ (212) 979-3000

Smithsonian National Associate Program
1100 Jefferson Drive SW, Room 3077
Washington, DC 20560
☎ (202) 357-4700

Diving tours:
Scuba Voyages
595 Fairbanks Street, Corona, CA 91719
☎ (800) 544-7631
(tours to Little Cayman and Cayman Brac only)

Tropical Adventures
111 Second Avenue N., Seattle, WA 98109
☎ (800) 247-3483

Family-oriented tour packages:
Rascals in Paradise
650 5th Street, Suite 505, San Francisco, CA 94107
☎ (800) 872-7225

Car Rental

Renting a vehicle, at least for part of your stay, is often the easiest and most economical way to get around, especially if you plan to explore. Car rentals begin at about US $30 per day; expect to pay about $43 per day for a 4x4 vehicle.

A temporary driver's license is required. You can obtain this from the rental agency by presenting a valid driver's license and paying the US $7.50 fee. You must also show a major credit card. You must be 21 or over to rent a vehicle; some agencies require renters to be 25 years of age.

Jeeps are popular rentals here.

Remember that driving is on the **left** side throughout the Cayman Islands. Most vehicles are right-hand drive; most 4x4s have a left-hand stick shift.

CAR RENTAL AGENCIES

In George Town:

Andy's Rent A Car, Airport Rd.	☎ (345) 949-5579
Budget Rent A Car, Walkers Rd.	☎ (345) 949-5605
Cayman Rentals, N. Church St.	☎ (345) 949-6408
Coconut Car Rentals, Crewe Rd.	☎ (800) 262-6687
	or (345) 949-4377
Conmac Car Rental, Airport Rd.	☎ (345) 949-6955
E. Scott Rent A Car, Airport Centre	☎ (345) 949-8867
Economy, Biggies Pl., Airport Rd.	☎ (345) 949-9550
Just Jeeps, N. Church. St.	☎ (345) 949-7263
K&K, Rankins Pl., Eastern Ave.	☎ (345) 949-7857
Soto's 4X4 Ltd.	☎ (345) 945-2420
(Mary St. north of cruise ship landing)	
Tropical, Rankins Pl., Eastern Ave.	☎ (345) 949-1950

At the airport:

Cico/Avis	☎ (345) 949-2468
Budget	☎ (345) 949-5605
Coconut Car Rentals	☎ (800) 262-6687
	or (345) 949-7703
Dollar Rent-A-Car	☎ (345) 949-4790
Economy	☎ (345) 949-9550
Hertz	☎ (345) 949-2280
Marshall's Rent A Car	☎ (345) 949-7821
National	☎ (345) 949-4790
Soto's 4x4 Ltd.	☎ (345) 945-1232
Thrifty	☎ (800) FOR-CARS
	or (345) 949-6640

Seven Mile Beach:

Andy's Rent A Car (opp. Marriott)	☎ (345) 949-8111
Avis Cico Rent A Car	
(Hyatt Regency location)	☎ (345) 949-8468
(Westin Casuarina location)	☎ (345) 945-5585
Coconut Car Rentals, Coconut Pl.	☎ (800) 262-6687
	or (345) 949-4377
Hertz Rent-A-Car, Marriott Hotel	☎ (345) 949-8147
Marshall's	☎ (345) 949-2127

(Turtle Beach Villas, West Bay Rd.)
Soto's 4x4 Ltd.   ☎ (345) 945-2424
    (2 blocks north of Marriott)
Sunshine Car Rentals, West Bay Rd. ☎ (345) 949-3858

Cayman Brac:
Avis/Cico   ☎ (345) 948-2847
Brac-Hertz Rent-a-Car   ☎ (345) 948-1515
Four D's Car Rental   ☎ (345) 948-1599

Little Cayman:
McLaughlin Car Rentals   ☎ (345) 948-1000

Taxi Service

Taxi rates are based on a maximum of three riders. The minimum fee is CI $4 for the first mile, CI $1.75 for each additional mile. Waiting time is charged at CI $.75 per minute. All prices below are given in CI dollars.

Airport to Hyatt	$11.20
Lighthouse (East End) to Westin Casuarina	$32.25
George Town to Treasure Isle Resort	$5.50
George Town to Villas of the Galleon	$8.00
Sleep Inn to Westin Casuarina	$6.50
Sleep Inn to Turtle Farm	$14.50
Westin to Turtle Farm	$11.00
Treasure Isle Resort to Hell	$12.75

On Foot

With the low crime rate in the Cayman Islands, travel on foot is fun, safe, and easy. Walking is the easiest way to get around George Town, especially along the waterfront area. Many travelers also walk along Seven Mile Beach, strolling to dinner and back to their hotel. If you are staying in the East End or West Bay, however, consider another transportation option.

Travel Information

NOTE: *Driving is on the left side throughout the Cayman Islands, so pedestrians should always look **right** before crossing the street.*

Scooters

Scooters are available for rent at two locations on Grand Cayman. **Cayman Cycle Rentals** (☎ 345-945-4021) has rentals at Treasure Island Resort, the Hyatt Regency Grand Cayman, and Coconut Place; **Soto Sooters and Car Rentals** (☎ 345-945-4652) at Coconut Place also offers rentals. Scooters average about $25 per day. A permit is required to drive a scooter and riding experience is necessary.

Bicycles

With its relatively flat grade, the Cayman Islands are a good destination for bicyclists. On Grand Cayman, along West Bay Road, traffic can be extremely heavy during morning and evening rush hours.

For rentals on Grand Cayman, call **Cayman Cycle Rentals** at ☎ (345) 945-4021 or stop by the offices at Coconut Place on West Bay Road, the Hyatt Regency Grand Cayman, or Treasure Island Resort, all on Seven Mile Beach. Bicycle rentals are also available from **Soto's Scooters and Car Rentals** at Coconut Place. ☎ (345) 945-4652.

Prices vary, but average about $12 per day for a 10-speed bike and $14 for a mountain bike.

On Little Cayman, bicycling is one of the best means of travel and complimentary bicycle use is available from most accommodations.

Guided Tours

Guided tours are a good way for first-time visitors to get a good overview of the nation. Guided tours are available from most taxi drivers for about US $37.50 per hour for four persons; you can also check with your hotel tour desk for possibilities. Island tours typically include the Cayman Turtle Farm, Hell, Seven Mile Beach, and other attractions. Prices start at US $25 for a two-hour tour and run up to about $66 for a full-day trip. Here are several tour operators that offer varying packages:

Burton's Tours
☎ (345) 949-7222, fax (345) 947-6222
Burton Ebanks is a local resident with an extensive knowledge of the entire region. He does both group and private tours and we can highly recommend him for his complete knowledge of Grand Cayman.

Elite Limousine Service
☎ (345) 947-2561, fax (345) 949-3834
Elite does both sightseeing tours as well as airport transfers.

Evco Tours
☎ (345) 949-2118, fax (345) 949-0137
Sightseeing tours, dinner cruises, cruise ship tours, charter fishing trips, and more handled by this agency.

Majestic Tours
☎ (345) 949-7773, fax (345) 949-8647
Aiport transfers and sightseeing tours.

McCurley's Tours
☎ (345) 947-9626
Sightseeing tours as well as transfers available.

Reids Premier Tours
☎ (345) 949-6531, fax (345) 949-4770
Sightseeing tours, shopping tours, fishing trips, snorkel trips, and more offered.

Travel Information

Rudy's Travellers Transport, West Bay
☎ (345) 949-3208, fax (345) 949-1155
Rudy Powery, president of the Bird Club, leads
guided birding tours as well as sightseeing trips.

Silver Thatch Excursions
☎ and fax (345) 945-6588
Both the history and natural history of the area can
be learned aboard a Silver Thatch Excursion. Six
different tours are available, including The
Eastern Experience (historic sites from Old
Prospect to the Ten Sails Monument in East End);
Walk the Mastic Trail; Botanic Park Adventures
(choice of Historic Route or Environmental
Route); A Walk Back In History (historic walking
tour of West Bay); Central George Town; Visit to
Old Prospect (Watler's Cemetery, Old Savannah
Schoolhouse). Birdwatching Excursions to one or
more natural wildlife habitats include the
Governor Michael Gore Bird Sanctuary; Meagre
Bay Pond; Botanic Park and Malportas Farm.
Hotel pickup/return, drink, and snack (sandwich
and traditional Caymanian pastries) are included.

Tropicana Tours Ltd.
☎ (345) 949-0944, fax (345) 949-4507
Sightseeing and watersports are handled by this
agency.

Vernon's Sightseeing Tours
☎ (345) 949-1509, fax (345) 949-0213
Sightseeing tours, dinner transfers, shopping
tours, fishing trips and more offered.

Accommodations

You'll find a wide variety of accommodations in the Cayman
Islands, especially on Grand Cayman. Luxury resorts, full-service
hotels, lavish condominiums, budget hotels, guest houses, and
bed-and-breakfasts are available.

Room prices vary greatly with type of accommodation, location, and time of year. High season (mid-December through mid-April) brings prices about 40% higher than in summer months. Government tax of 10% is charged on all accommodations.

Here are some average prices for a one-night stay during high season:

Seven Mile Beach resorts	$200-$300
Small hotels, inns	$175-$200
Condominiums	$95-$500
Guest houses	$60-$80
Villas	$300-$700
Cayman Brac properties	$85-$200
Little Cayman properties	$150-$400

To book condominiums and villas, call the property directly or one of the booking agencies that handles condominium and villa reservations:

International Travel & Resorts	☎ (800) 223-9815
Reef Fanta-Seas	☎ (800) 327-3835
Robert Reid Associates	☎ (800) 223-6510
Star Travel Ltd.	☎ (770) 493-1747
Cayman Kai Development Co.	☎ (800) 336-6008
Cayman Villas	☎ (800) 235-5888
Hibiscus Realty	☎ (345) 949-7429
Cayman Condo Holiday	☎ (800) 232-1034
Tradewinds Property Mgmt.	☎ (345) 947-3029
Tropical Property Mgmt.	☎ (345) 945-4787
Blossom Villas/McLaughlin Ent. (Little Cayman)	☎ (345) 948-1000

Special Concerns

Dress

Swimsuits are de rigueur on the beach, but wear a cover-up away from the sand and swimming pool. You will find that this is a casual island, however, and many restaurants welcome casual dress (shorts, t-shirts) at dinner. Call for dress recommendations if you have doubts.

Nude and topless sunbathing is prohibited throughout the Cayman Islands.

Crime

One of the Cayman Island's greatest assets is its low crime rate. With its excellent economic position, crime is rare. Vacationers and locals both enjoy walking on public beaches or strolling along busy West Bay Street after an evening meal.

Crime rates are especially low on Little Cayman. When you pick up your rental vehicle at the one agency in town, they'll tell you just to leave the keys in the ignition.

However, no destination is completely crime-free. Use the same common-sense precautions you would exercise at home.

◆ Do not leave valuables on the beach while swimming. Invest in a waterproof pouch for keys and necessities and lock other items in your car or hotel room.

◆ Don't leave valuables in your unlocked rental car. Many of the Cayman Islands' rental vehicles are open-air jeeps; leave possessions in your hotel room.

◆ Use hotel safes and safety deposit boxes.

◆ Don't walk in isolated areas alone at night.

Drugs

Be warned that the Cayman Islands exercise strict anti-drug laws. Marijuana is an illegal substance and possession of it can result not only in large fines but also in a prison term.

Marriage

Getting married in the Cayman Islands is now a simple process. Couples need to arrange for a Marriage Officer and must apply for a special marriage license for non-residents (US $200) at the Chief Secretary's office, Fourth Floor, Room 406, Government Administration Building, George Town, ☎ (345) 949-7900.

The simplest way to go about this is to contact the Chief Secretary's office before your visit to obtain the name of a Marriage Officer (who will need to be named on your application form). You'll then complete the form with your names, occupations, permanent addresses, and your temporary address while staying in the Cayman Islands. You will also need to present the following:

◆ Valid passports or birth certificates verifying that you are at least 18 years of age (the minimum age for marriage without parental consent).

◆ The original (or a certified copy) divorce decree or death certificate, if applicable.

◆ A letter from the authorized Marriage Officer who will officiate at your ceremony.

◆ A Cayman Islands International Immigration Department pink slip showing proof of entry. Or, for cruise passengers, a boarding pass. If you are arriving on a cruise ship, have your Purser call ahead to the ship's agent for assistance.

◆ Two witnesses.

No residency period is required. Write for a copy of the free brochure, *Getting Married in the Cayman Islands*, from Government Information Services, Broadcasting House, Grand Cayman, ☎ (345) 949-8092 or fax (345) 949-5936.

Travel Information

Water

Water throughout the Cayman Islands is drinkable, although many resorts use desalinated water produced by reverse osmosis. The result is safe, potable water, although some visitors prefer the taste of bottled water. You'll find bottled water available at restaurants and grocery stores throughout the islands.

Electricity

Electricity is 120 volts at 60 cycles. US appliances will not need adapters.

Gratuities

A 15% gratuity is standard. Some establishments add the gratuity to the bill automatically, so be sure to check first.

Telephone

Most 800 numbers will not work from the Cayman Islands. To access toll-free numbers, substitute 400 for 800. Callers are charged for these calls.

Time

Eastern Standard Time. The Cayman Islands do not observe daylight savings time. Locally, dial 844 for current time.

Clinics

For medical emergencies, you'll find a hospital on Grand Cayman and one on Cayman Brac:

Faith Hospital
Stake Bay, Cayman Brac
☎ (345) 948-2356

George Town Hospital
George Town, Grand Cayman
☎ (345) 949-8600

Several medical centers offer non-emergency care:

Cayman Medical and Surgical Centre
Rankin's Plaza, Eastern Avenue G
George Town
☎ (345) 949-8150

Professional Medical Centre
Walkers Road
George Town
☎ (345) 949-6066

West Bay Road Medical Clinic
West Bay Road (next to Treasure Island Resort)
Grand Cayman
☎ (345) 949-2080

Hyperbaric Chamber

A two-person, double-lock recompression chamber is available for emergency treatment on Grand Cayman at the George Town Hospital. It is staffed 24 hours a day by trained operators and supervised by a physician specializing in hyperbaric medicine.

Precautions

Remember when your mom told you "look but don't touch"? Those words of wisdom come in handy on the islands. Although most plants and animals are harmless, you'll find a few creepy crawlies both in and out of the water, as well as some plants that are best avoided.

Travel Information

SCORPIONFISH: A mottled pinkish fish that hangs out on coral and is so ugly it actually looks dangerous.

SEA URCHINS: Painful if you step on their brittle spines.

JELLYFISH: These cause painful stings with their tentacles.

STINGRAYS: Dangerous if stepped on. Can be avoided by dragging your feet when wading, which kicks up the sand.

FIRE CORAL: There are many varieties. All those edged in white will burn you if you brush against them.

NO-SEE-UMS: Tucked into that oh-so-wonderful sand lie tiny sand fleas, waiting to bite when the sand cools. You won't feel their bites, but just wait a day or two: welts like jumbo mosquito bites will make themselves apparent and they'll itch for days. To avoid the no-see-ums, stay off the sand at sunset. The fleas are most active when the sand cools.

MANCHINEEL: Manchineel trees (*Hippomane mancinella*) present an unusual danger. These plants, members of the Spurge plant family, have highly acidic leaves and fruit. During a rain, water dropping off the leaves can cause painful burns on your skin and the tree's tiny apples will also burn when stepped on. In most resorts, manchineel trees have been removed or are clearly marked, often with signs and with trunks painted red.

COWITCH (*Mucuna pruriens* and *Helicteres jamaicensis*): Think of fiberglass on a vine. Think how much you'd itch if you brushed into this plant, covered with fine fibers, as you walked along in shorts. Think of avoiding this one.

COCKSPUR (*Caesalpinia bonduc*): This shrub won't inflict any permanent damage, but it will rip at you with its hooked thorns as you walk past.

MAIDEN PLUM (*Comocladia dentata*): Be prepared for a nasty rash from this weed if you come in contact with its sap. The weed is dark green with ovate-shaped leaves.

SAND SPURS (*Cenchrus genus*): Also called "wait-a-minute," this pesky thorn will penetrate unsuspecting bare feet that stumble across it in the sand. Best defense: follow mom's advice once again and wear your shoes.

SNAKES: The Cayman Islands do not have any poisonous snake species. You might come across a harmless grass snake (*Alsophis* *cantherigerus*), which feeds on frogs and lizards. The population of this reptile has been reduced by mongooses on the island.

SUNBURN: Nothing will slow down your vacation faster than a sunburn, your biggest danger in the Caribbean. You'll be surprised, even if you don't burn easily or if you already have a good base tan, how easily the sun sneaks up on you. At this southern latitude, good sunscreen, applied liberally and often, is a must. This ailment ranks as the number one travelers' concern throughout the Caribbean. You are especially vulnerable while on the water; sea breezes may cool the skin but don't prevent burns. Many snorkelers wear t-shirts to protect exposed backs from these strong rays.

Sunscreens are sold on all the islands, but prices are steep; plan ahead and bring your favorite brand from home.

RAINY DAY ACTIVITIES

Into every vacation a little rain may fall, so if clouds prevail during your vacation, don't despair. Here's a list of activities that don't depend on sunshine:

- ◆ Cayman Turtle Farm (Grand Cayman's West Bay area). Although much of the farm is located outdoors, the tanks can be enjoyed in all but the worst weather.
- ◆ National Museum (George Town).
- ◆ Scuba diving.
- ◆ Shopping in George Town.
- ◆ Pirate Cave, Grand Cayman.
- ◆ Caves, Cayman Brac.
- ◆ *Seaworld Explorer* (George Town).
- ◆ *Atlantis Submarine* (George Town).
- ◆ Cardinal D's Park, George Town.

Note that most tropical rainstorms are short-lived.

Travel Information

Information Sources

When on Grand Cayman, visit the **Cayman Islands Department of Tourism** office at Elgin Avenue, Cricket Square, in George Town, ☎ (345) 949-0623, fax (345) 949-4053. You'll also find information booths with maps and brochures at the Owen Roberts International Airport and the North Terminal cruise ship dock.

Before your trip, contact the tourism office nearest you for brochures and information. For general information and reservations, call the Cayman Islands Department of Tourism at ☎ (800) 346-3313. For hotel and condo rates in the Cayman Islands and for special air-accommodation packages, ☎ (800) G-CAYMAN, the number of the Cayman Airways Holidays.

TOURISM OFFICES

Miami: 6100 Blue Lagoon Drive, Suite 150, Miami, FL 33126-2085, ☎ (305) 266-2300

New York: 420 Lexington Avenue, Suite 2733, New York, NY 10170; ☎ (212) 682-5582

Houston: Two Memorial City Plaza, 820 Gessner, Suite 170, Houston, TX 77024; ☎ (713) 461-1317

Los Angeles: 3440 Wilshire Boulevard, Suite 1202, Los Angeles, CA 90010; ☎ (213) 738-1968

Chicago: 9525 W. Bryn Mawr Avenue, Suite 160, Rosemont, Il 60018; ☎ (708) 678-6446

Canada: 234 Eglinton Avenue East, Suite 306, Toronto, Ontario, Canada M4P 1K5; ☎ (416) 485-1550

United Kingdom: 6 Arlington Street, London, SW1A 1Re, England, United Kingdom; ☎ (0171) 491-7771

While on-island, pick up a copy of the free *Key* or *Destination Cayman* magazines for information on shopping, dining, and nightly entertainment. *What to Do Cayman* and *What's Hot! in Cayman* look at places of interest to visitors. Another good source of information is the Cayman Airways in-flight magazine, *Horizons*. These publications are distributed at the Owen Roberts International Airport as well as at most hotels. Grand Cayman has a daily paper, *The Caymanian Compass*.

Three local television stations serve the Cayman Islands. CITN (channel 27), CTS (channel 24) and CCT, Cayman Christian Television (channel 21), provide local broadcasting. Most residents and practically all resorts and hotels receive satellite television broadcasts from the States.

Three local radio stations broadcast in the islands. Radio Cayman, owned by the government, is broadcast on all the islands. Z-99 and ICCI-FM at the International College of the Cayman Islands broadcast on Grand Cayman.

INTERNET SITE: Check out the Cayman Islands Web site on the internet at http://www.caymans.com for lots of helpful information, current weather, news, and more.

Travel Information

Where Are The Adventures?

The Cayman Islands present a variety of adventure opportunities, no matter what your fitness or activity level. Adventures both on land and in water are available.

On Foot

Walking & Hiking

 With its flat grade, walking is a popular activity on all three Cayman Islands. Except along West Bay Road, parallel to Seven Mile Beach, and in George Town, there's very little traffic to contend with and plenty to see. Walking is a good way to meet local residents; it's traditional to greet others with "Good morning" or "Good afternoon" and a smile.

Hikers will also find marked trails. The Mastic Trail on the East End of Grand Cayman is the newest offering (see the *East of George Town* chapter for more on this trail, which features several eco-areas on a guided walk). Another excellent hike, this one self-guided, is found at the Botanic Garden, also discussed in the *East of George Town* section.

> **NOTE:** *Mid-day heat can be intense, especially once you enter the interior of the island away from the cooling tradewinds. Always carry water with you and be aware of heat exhaustion and sunstroke.*

Underwater

Scuba Diving

The Cayman Islands are universally recognized as a top dive destination. Since 1957, with the founding of the Caribbean's first dive operation on Grand Cayman, these islands have caught the attention of the diving world. Bob Soto established that first operation and today over 40 such establishments provide service on the three islands.

Diving in the Cayman Islands.

Today, the Cayman Islands Watersports Operators Association (CIWOA) estimates that about one third of all overnight visitors are scuba divers and about 80% enjoy some form of watersports during their stay (plus, about a fourth of the cruise ship passengers enjoy watersports). The numbers continue to grow but, because of the large number of dive sites in these islands, visitors can still enjoy a feeling of discovery. Strict marine laws protect the beautiful reefs and ensure pristine dive sites.

Just why is Cayman such a popular dive destination? The reasons are many.

◆   Dive sites start close to shore in shallow water (25 to 60 feet).

◆ A variety of dive experiences is available, for beginners as well as advanced divers.

◆ Quality dive operations are found throughout the islands.

◆ Instruction is readily available through any of the certification agencies (PADI, NAUI, SSI, NASDS, and YMCA).

◆ Green sea turtles are often sighted on dives.

◆ Scuba instruction is available in many languages; Much of the marine life is approachable, such as the rays at Stingray City.

◆ Visibility is excellent year-round.

◆ A leeward side of each island ensures calm water (dive operations are so confident of this that many guarantee diving 365 days a year)

◆ Strict conservation laws have protected the reefs.

◆ The Caribbean's oldest underwater photography school is located here.

◆ A hyperbaric recompression chamber is available 24 hours a day.

Over 200 sites lure divers of all abilities, from beginners looking for shore excursions and shallow reef dives to advanced divers seeking wreck and cave explorations. You'll find professional assistance from dive operators on each of the three islands. These incluse resort courses, where you can sample diving after a one-day course; full certification courses, which will award you a "c" card; and advanced courses to teach you the use of scuba computers, the skills of drift diving, and even underwater photography.

Incredible visibility, measured at 100 to 150 feet, helps make these islands such spectacular dive destinations. With year-round water temperatures of 77 to 83°, visitors can dive comfortably and enjoy an underwater playground that's filled with marine life.

Grand Cayman offers approximately 130 dive spots, many less than half a mile from shore. The island is surrounded by approximately 60 miles of drop-offs. One of the most popular shallow dive sites is Stingray City on the North Sound. This 12-foot dive is

Adventures

memorable for the southern Atlantic stingrays that divers and snorkelers can feed by hand.

Cayman Brac also offers drop-offs as well as coral gardens and caves. Little Cayman is especially noted for Bloody Bay Wall, a drop-off that begins at just 18 feet below the surface and plunges to over 1,000 feet. Visibility here often ranges to 200 feet.

The appeal of these dive sites has been maintained even in the face of rising tourism and an increasing number of divers. Strict marine conservation laws ensure the safety of the reefs and the marine life. Dive sites are protected with permanent moorings (over 200 in the islands) so boats can moor rather than anchor and risk damage to the fragile reefs.

To protect both the safety of the reefs and the divers who come to this island, the Cayman Islands watersports operators adhere to strict regulations. The Cayman Islands Watersports Operators Association (CIWOA) was founded in 1981 to ensure the safety of the divers and the reefs. Members emphasize good neutral buoyancy techniques to prevent damage to the corals because of improper positioning in the water. Also, CIWOA dive boats visit only those sites with moorings installed by the Department of the Environment's Protection and Conservation unit.

EARTH WATCH: *Every year, members of CIWOA organize and participate in reef and ocean floor clean-up projects. The organization also works to make young Caymanians more aware of the local diving industry and to consider a career in the field by offering free PADI certification courses and snorkeling lessons for local schoolchildren and scout groups during special programs. Call the CIWOA at ☎ (345) 949-8522 for more information.*

Divers who want to advance their skills will also find technical instruction on Grand Cayman. **Divetech Ltd.,** ☎ (345) 916-3582, offers technical diving instruction, including certification in the use of Nitrox/EANx. Nitrox is a combination of nitrogen and oxygen that has long been used by military and technical divers and has now been approved for use by the Cayman Islands Watersports

Operators Association. Typical air has 79% nitrogen and 21% oxygen. Combinations with a greater percentage of oxygen are called Enriched Air Nitrox (EANx). The EANx mixture has 36% oxygen and is often used for cave and wreck diving.

This mixture also increases the safety factor, making the nitrogen accumulation the same as for a dive in waters 10 to 20 feet shallower. It reduces both the possibility of decompression sickness and fatigue following a dive. Also, divers can enjoy more bottom time with no decompression and a shorter decompression time beyond those limits. These factors make it desirable for divers not in peak physical condition and for older divers.

To use EANx, you must be a certified advanced open-water diver with a minimum of 10 open-water dives logged. The course for EANx use runs about US $220, including four hours of classroom instruction and two EANx dives.

Divetech Ltd. also offers rebreather certification. Rebreathers offer divers a silent dive with no bubbles or noise and are available for rent to divers certified in their use.

To share the company of other divers, contact the **British Sub Aqua Club** (Cayman Islands Divers, branch #360 BSAC, P.O. Box 1515 GT, Grand Cayman, ☎ 345-949-0685/ 949-2989). Visiting divers are welcome to join activities.

> **NOTE:** *The "Diver Down" red and white flag is required throughout the Cayman Islands for both divers and snorkelers in the water outside an identified swimming area.*

Dive Operators

Diving in the Cayman Islands is taken seriously as a business and the operators here are excellent, upholding the highest safety standards. Two local organizations, Cayman Islands Watersports Operators Association and the Cayman National Watersports Association, help maintain the excellent professional level.

We've listed dive operators throughout the islands. With Grand Cayman's small size, many divers are picked up by complimentary shuttles from operators on other parts of the island.

Adventures

Grand Cayman

Ambassador Divers, George Town
☎ (800) 648-7748
This PADI affiliated operation specializes in computer diving. They offer four daily dives on a 12-person boat.

Aquanauts Ltd., Seven Mile Beach
☎ (800) 357-2212
With PADI, NAUI, and SSI affiliations, this operator offers four daily dives on a 16-person boat. Instruction and customized dive packages available.

Bob Soto's Diving, Seven Mile Beach
☎ (800) BOB-SOTO
The Cayman Islands' first dive operator, in business since 1957, this company has five Seven Mile Beach locations. Grand Cayman's only PADI 5-Star Development Center. Also affiliated with NAUI, SSI, NASDS, and YMCA. Nine daily dives offered.

Calico Jack's Pirates Emporium, George Town
☎ (345) 949-4373
Located at the restaurant of the same name, this new operator is PADI affiliated. Certification courses, resort courses, day and night dives, and snorkel trips offered, as well as gear and camera rentals.

Capitol's Surfside, Seven Mile Beach
☎ (800) 543-6828
In business for nearly three decades, this operator runs two dives daily. PADI, NAUI, and SSI affiliated.

Capt. Marvin's Aquatics, West Bay
☎ (345) 945-4590
For over four decades Captain Marvin's has offered all levels of diving. PADI affiliated, the shop does three dives daily on a 40-person boat.

Cayman Dive College, Seven Mile Beach
☎ (345) 949-4125
This teaching facility offers instruction in English, German, French, Spanish, and Japanese. In operation 15 years and PADI affiliated.

Cayman Diving Lodge, East End
☎ (800) TLC-DIVE
For 25 years, this small diving lodge has offered East End diving, including one- and two-tank dives, night dives, and instruction. PADI affiliated.

Cayman Diving School, George Town
☎ (345) 949-4729
Specializing in instruction, this school caters to all skill levels, from resort to dive master. The PADI, SSI, and YMCA affiliated operation has been in business for 11 years.

Cayman Marine Lab, Seven Mile Beach
☎ (345) 916-0849
A 10-person capacity boat does three dives daily at this operation specializing in small charters. Also offers marine lectures for undersea awareness and appreciation programs. NAUI affiliated.

Celebrity Divers, George Town
☎ (345) 949-3410
This small operation specializes in small groups with a boat capacity of 10 divers. PADI and NAUI affiliated.

Crosby Ebanks C&G Watersports
Seven Mile Beach at Coconut Place
☎ (345) 945-4049
This operation has been in business over 36 years. Two daily dives on a boat capable of taking 50 divers. They offer a Stingray City dive and a snorkel trip as well as gear rental. PADI affiliated.

Dive Inn Ltd., Seven Mile Beach
☎ (800) 322-0321
For a decade this operation has run dives for all skill levels. Four dives daily are offered from a 12-person capacity boat. PADI and NAUI affiliated.

Divetech/Turtle Reef Divers, Seven Mile Beach
☎ (345) 949-1700
Specialty and technical training (including Nitrox) are available at this new operation. Certification, resort course, and night dives offered. PADI and NAUI affiliated.

Dive Time Ltd., George Town
☎ (345) 947-2339
For 17 years, this PADI and NAUI affiliated operation has offered four dives daily, including Stingray City, night dives, and more. Certification and resort courses offered. A six-person capacity boat keeps the trips small.

Divers Down
☎ (345) 945-1611
This new operation is PADI affiliated and runs two dives daily. Nitrox certification courses are available.

Divers Supply, Seven Mile Beach
☎ (345) 949-7621
This PADI operation has certification and resort courses, as well as Stingray City and night dives.

Don Foster's Dive Cayman Ltd., Seven Mile Beach
☎ (800) 83-DIVER
This operator is PADI, NAUI, YMCA, and SSI affiliated and offers three dives daily. Their boat has a capacity of 20 divers.

Eden Rock Diving Center Ltd., George Town
☎ (345) 949-7243
With its proximity to the cruise ship terminal, this is a popular operation that's been in business 13 years. Unlimited shore diving available to some of George Town's best sites. PADI, NAUI, and SSI affiliated.

Fisheye, Seven Mile Beach
☎ (800) 887-8569
This operator has three custom-built boats and operates a complete underwater photography operation with rentals, processing, and repairs. PADI, NAUI, and YMCA affiliated.

Indies Divers, Seven Mile Beach
☎ (800) 654-3130
There is a 12-diver maximum with this PADI affiliated operator. Three dives daily.

Neptune's Realm Divers, Seven Mile Beach
☎ (345) 949-6444
Small groups of up to eight divers accommodated by this PADI, NAUI, SSI, and NASDS affiliated operation. Five dives daily.

Nitrox Divers, George Town
☎ (345) 945-2064
This is the only operation dedicated to Nitrox diving, with Nitrox and IANTD certification courses. Maximum of eight divers per trip accepted at this PADI affiliated operation.

Adventures

Ocean Frontiers, East End
☎ (345) 947-7500
This new operator offers free shuttle service to its East End location. Two dives daily. PADI affiliated.

Off the Wall Divers, Seven Mile Beach
☎ (345) 947-7790
For five years, this operation has offered a variety of dives to small groups of up to 10. PADI and NAUI affiliated.

Ollen Miller's Sun Divers, Seven Mile Beach
☎ (345) 947-6606
Groups of up to eight divers are accommodated by this PADI affiliated shop that offers three dives daily.

Parrots Landing, George Town
☎ (800) 448-0428
This large operation has a fleet of seven dive boats as well as good shore diving just south of the cruise ship terminals. Six dives daily; PADI, NAUI, SSI, and NASDS affiliated.

Peter Milburn's Dive Cayman, Seven Mile Beach
☎ (345) 945-5770
For 18 years this operator has run dives for many skill levels. Three dives daily. PADI, NAUI, SSI, NASDS, and YMCA affiliated.

Quabbin Dives, George Town
☎ (800) 238-6712
For 17 years this operator has offered a variety of dives; the boat capacity is 30 divers. PADI, NAUI, and SSI affiliated.

Quabo Dives, George Town
☎ (345) 945-4769
Offering North Wall and West Wall dives, this PADI, SSI, and YMCA affiliated operator accommodates small groups.

Red Sail Sports, Seven Mile Beach
☎ (800) 255-6425
Located adjacent to the Hyatt Regency Grand Cayman, this operator has three dives daily with a boat capacity of 24. Complete dive packages available. PADI, NAUI, SSI, and NASDS affiliated.

Resort Sports Ltd., Seven Mile Beach and West Bay
☎ (800) 482-DIVE
Located at the Beach Club Colony and the Spanish Bay Reef hotels, this operator has been in business 10 years. PADI, NAUI and SSI affiliated, they do two dives daily for a capacity of 16 divers.

River Sports Divers Ltd.
Seven Mile Beach at Coconut Place
☎ (345) 949-1181
All levels of divers are accommodated in groups no larger than 14. PADI and SSI affiliated.

Seasports, West Bay
☎ (345) 949-3965
For 24 years Seasports has catered to small groups, only two to eight divers per boat. Pickup by boat from hotels and condos along Seven Mile Beach. PADI and NAUI affiliated.

7-Mile Watersports, Seven Mile Beach
☎ (345) 949-0332
Certification and resort courses as well as various dives. PADI and NAUI affiliated operator.

Adventures

Scuba Sensations, Seven Mile Beach
☎ (800) 767-0445
Located at Treasure Island Resort, Scuba Sensations takes divers to walls and wrecks around the island. PADI, NAUI, and SSI affiliated.

Soto's Cruises, Seven Mile Beach
☎ (345) 945-4576
This 20-person capacity operation caters to advanced certified divers. PADI affiliated.

Sunset Divers, George Town
☎ (800) 854-4767
At Sunset House. This 25-year operation has at least two daily dives as well as offshore diving at Sunset Reef. PADI, NAUI, SSI, and NASDS affiliated.

Tortuga Divers Ltd., East End
☎ (345) 947-2097
Located at Morritt's Tortuga Club, this operator has taken out divers for 20 years. PADI affiliated.

Treasure Island Divers, George Town
☎ (800) 872-7552
Behind Treasure Island Resort, this 10-year-old facility has two dives daily. PADI, NAUI, and SSI affiliated.

Cayman Brac

Brac Aquatics Ltd.
☎ (800) 544-BRAC
For 20 years this operator has offered dives for all skill levels. Three dives daily with a 14-diver maximum. PADI and NAUI affiliated.

Peter Hughes Dive Tiara
☎ (800) 367-3484
This PADI 5-star dive and photo center leads visits to over 50 sites on Cayman Brac and neighboring Little Cayman. Located at the Divi Tiara Beach Resort, it has photo and video rentals. PADI, NAUI, SSI, and NASDS affiliated.

Reef Divers
☎ (800) 327-3835
Located at Brac Reef Beach Resort, this dive service includes a full-service photo and video center. Three dives daily with a 20-person maximum. PADI, NAUI, SSI, and NASDS affiliated.

Little Cayman

Paradise Divers
☎ (800) 450-2084
Groups of up to 16 accommodated by this facility, with three dives daily. Complimentary beverages. PADI affiliated.

Pirates Point Resort
☎ (800) 327-8777
Located at Pirates Point Resort, this shop offers two dives daily for groups up to 20 divers. PADI, NAUI, and SSI affiliated.

Reef Divers
☎ (800) 327-3835
Little Cayman Beach Resort is home to this facility, which includes a full-service photo and video center. Three dives daily for groups of up to 20 divers. PADI, NAUI, SSI, and NASDS affiliated.

Sam McCoy's Fishing & Diving Lodge
☎ (800) 626-0496
Located on Little Cayman's north shore, this operator offers excursions to the Bloody Bay Wall

Adventures

as well as shore diving along Jackson's Point.
PADI and NAUI affiliated.

Southern Cross Club
☎ (800) 899-2582
This fishing and diving resort has four dives daily
for small groups (no more than 10 divers). PADI,
NAUI, and SSI affiliated.

Liveaboards

For those divers who want to eat, sleep, and drink diving, the
liveaboard is a good choice. You'll spend a week with others who
share your interest. There's no need to waste time reaching dive
sites; what seems like your personal yacht for the week just whisks
you there.

Cayman Aggressor III
☎ (800) 348-2628
This George Town-based liveaboard has five
professional staff members and a maximum of 16
guests. In operation for 12 years, it is PADI, NAUI,
SSI, NASDS, and YMCA affiliated and offers
photo and video rentals. Divers enjoy sites off all
three islands. The all-inclusive cost of a week's
stay runs $1,495.

Little Cayman Diver II
☎ (800) 458-BRAC
Based off Little Cayman, this liveaboard
accommodates 10 passengers in five cabins, each
with a private bath. PADI, NAUI, SSI, NASDS,
and YMCA affiliated, this operator has been in
business for 10 years. Video rentals available. The
cost of a one-week all-inclusive stay is
$1,395-$1,595.

Tethered Scuba

For those curious about the undersea world but not ready to take the plunge for a full certification course, two outfits offer a tethered scuba experience to depths of 20 feet (see *Adventures, George Town,* page 108).

Submarines

For underwater fun, *Atlantis Submarine* and *Seaworld Explorer* provide a peek at the marine world (see *Adventures, George Town*). *Atlantis* plunges to a depth of 100 feet below the surface; *Seaworld Explorer* is a semi-submersible similar to a glass-bottom boat.

Underwater Photography

As home of the Caribbean's oldest underwater photography school, Grand Cayman draws many beginning and advanced underwater photographers. One of the Caribbean's best known underwater photographers, Cathy Church, operates Cathy Church's Underwater Photo Centre at Sunset House Resort in George Town. Classes, rentals, and processing services are available.

Underwater Photography Centers

Here's a list of underwater photography centers in the Cayman Islands. Stop here to rent underwater camera equipment, take lessons, or to have your shots developed.

Grand Cayman

Cathy Church's Sunset Underwater Photo Centre
Sunset House Hotel, South Church Street and
Coconut Place on West Bay Road
☎ (345) 949-7415, fax (345) 949-9770

Adventures

Divers Supply
West Shore Centre on West Bay Road
☎ (345) 949-4373, fax (345) 949-0294

Don Foster's Ocean Photo
Seven Mile Beach
☎ (345) 946-6607

Parrot's Landing Underwater Photo Centre
South Church St.
☎ (345) 949-7884

Fisheye Photographic Services
Cayman Falls on West Bay Rd.
☎ (345) 945-4209, fax (345) 949-4208

Cayman Brac

Brac Photographics Ltd.
(next to Brac Reef Resort)
☎ (345) 948-1340

Reef Photo Video Center
Brac Reef Beach Resort
☎ (345) 948-1323, fax (345) 948-1207

Little Cayman

Reef Photo & Video Centre &
Little Cayman Beach Resort
☎ (345) 948-1033, fax (345) 948-1040

And if you're not ready to gear up with the full underwater photography outfit, at least buy a disposable underwater camera. These generally work to a depth of 15 feet and are perfect for capturing a few memories of snorkel trips, Stingray City, and the underwater beauty of the Cayman Islands.

Snorkeling

If scuba diving is not for you, consider snorkeling. Many of Cayman's scenic reefs can be enjoyed in water just a few feet deep with equipment as limited as a mask and a snorkel. Snorkeling is an excellent introduction to the underwater beauty and rich marine life found in the Cayman waters. Just yards from shore, you can enjoy a look at colorful corals, graceful fans, and fish that include friendly sergeant majors, butterfly fish, and shy damselfish.

And don't feel that wreck diving is just for scuba divers. In Grand Cayman snorkelers can also enjoy a look at a wreck just a short swim from George Town's shores. The *Cali* sits in shallow water and is an easy snorkel trip. (See *George Town*, page 107.) Most resorts offer snorkel equipment at little or no charge.

> **TIP:** *To prevent your mask from fogging, rub saliva on the inside of the lens. Dishwashing liquid and special alcohol-based non-fogging formulas may also be used.*

Snorkel trips are also offered by many dive operators, the most popular being the excursion to Stingray City (see *West Bay* chapter for more on the island's top attraction and a list of operators that offer snorkel trips to the site). Typically, these trips include drinks and often lunch following the snorkeling adventure.

Snorkel Operators

The following list of operators offer guided half- and/or full-day snorkel excursions. Most include equipment; some include beverages and lunch. Complimentary shuttle services may also be offered.

Grand Cayman

Abanks Watersports & Tours Ltd., Seven Mile Beach,
☎ (345) 945-1444
Ambassador Divers, George Town, ☎ (800) 648-7748
Aquanauts Ltd., Seven Mile Beach, ☎ (800) 357-2212

Bayside Watersports, Ltd., Seven Mile Beach, ☎ (345) 949-1750
Black Princess Charters, Seven Mile Beach,
  ☎ (345) 949-0400/3821
Bob Soto's Diving, Seven Mile Beach, ☎ (800) BOB-SOTO
Calico Jack's Pirates Emporium, George Town,
  ☎ (345) 949-4373
Capitol's Surfside, Seven Mile Beach, ☎ (800) 543-6828
Capt. Marvin's Aquatics, West Bay, ☎ (345) 945-4590
Cayman Delight Cruises, West Bay, ☎ (345) 949-8111
Cayman Marine Lab, Seven Mile Beach, ☎ (345) 916-0849
Cayman Sunset, Seven Mile Beach, ☎ (345) 949-3666/3948
Celebrity Divers, George Town, ☎ (345) 949-3410
Charter Boat Headquarters, Seven Mile Beach,
  ☎ (345) 945-4340
Crosby Ebanks C&G Watersports
  Seven Mile Beach at Coconut Place, ☎ (345) 945-4049
Deep Sea Fox, George Town, ☎ (345) 945-4340
Dive Inn Ltd., Seven Mile Beach, ☎ (800) 322-0321
Divetech Ltd./Turtle Reef Divers, Seven Mile Beach,
  ☎ (345) 949-1700
Dive Time Ltd., George Town, ☎ (345) 947-2339
Divers Down, ☎ (345) 945-1611
Divers Supply, Seven Mile Beach, ☎ (345) 949-7621
Don Foster's Dive Cayman Ltd., Seven Mile Beach,
  ☎ (800) 83-DIVER
Eden Rock Diving Center Ltd., George Town, ☎ (345) 949-7243
Fisheye, Seven Mile Beach, ☎ (800) 887-8569
Frank's Watersports, Seven Mile Beach, ☎ (345) 945-5491
Indies Divers, Seven Mile Beach, ☎ (800) 654-3130
Island Girl Charts, George Town, ☎ (345) 947-3029
Jackie's Watersports, West Bay, ☎ (345) 945-5791
Kelly's Watersports, West Bay, ☎ (345) 949-1193/1509
Kirk Sea Tours, Ltd., George Town, ☎ (345) 949-6986
Ocean Frontiers, East End, ☎ (345) 947-7500
Ocean Safari, Ltd., George Town, ☎ (345) 945-1611
Off the Wall Divers, Seven Mile Beach, ☎ (345) 947-7790
Oh Boy Charters, West Bay, ☎ (345) 949-6341
Ollen Miller's Sun Divers, Seven Mile Beach, ☎ (345) 947-6606
Parrots Landing, George Town, ☎ (800) 448-0428
Peacemaker Charters, Seven Mile Beach, ☎ (345) 916-2478
Peter Milburn's Dive Cayman Ltd., Seven Mile Beach,
  ☎ (345) 945-5770
Quabbin Dives, George Town, ☎ (800) 238-6712

Quabo Dives, George Town, ☎ (345) 945-4769
Red Sail Sports, Seven Mile Beach, ☎ (800) 255-6425
Resort Sports Ltd., Seven Mile Beach and West Bay,
    ☎ (800) 482-DIVE
River Sports Divers Ltd., Seven Mile Beach at Coconut Place,
    ☎ (345) 949-1181
Seasports, West Bay, ☎ (345) 949-3965
Sunlight Charters, George Town, ☎ (345) 945-4340
7-Mile Watersports, Seven Mile Beach, ☎ (345) 949-0332
Scuba Sensations, Seven Mile Beach, ☎ (800) 767-0445
Soto's Cruises, Seven Mile Beach, ☎ (345) 945-4576
Temptress, Seven Mile Beach, ☎ (345) 949-0400
Tortuga Divers Ltd., East End, ☎ (345) 947-2097
Tourist Information & Activity Services, Seven Mile Beach,
    ☎ (345) 949-6598
Treasure Island Divers, George Town, ☎ (800) 872-7552
Wet 'n' Wild Watersports, Seven Mile Beach, ☎ (345) 949-9180

Cayman Brac

Brac Aquatics Ltd., ☎ (800) 544-BRAC
Peter Hughes Dive Tiara, ☎ (800) 367-3484
Reef Divers, ☎ (800) 327-3835

Little Cayman

Paradise Divers, ☎ (800) 450-2084
Pirates Point Resort, ☎ (800) 327-8777
Reef Divers, ☎ (800) 327-3835
Sam McCoy's Fishing & Diving Lodge, ☎ (800) 626-0496
Southern Cross Club, ☎ (800) 899-2582

Swimming

If swimming's your thing, call the Stingray Swim Club of Cayman
(☎ 345-949-8105). The club hosts several competitions and visitors
are welcome to participate in local events.

Adventures

UNDERWATER ADVENTURE COSTS

These costs represent average prices for underwater activities (in US dollars):

Snorkel trip	$25-$30
Stingray City snorkel trip	$25-$45
Snorkel equipment rental	$5-$8
Half-day snorkel trip	$20-$35
Full-day snorkel trip	$38-$45
Stingray City dive	$45-$50
One-tank dive	$35-$45
Two-tank dive	$55-$65
Night dive	$25-$50
Resort course	$75-$90
Scuba certification course	$250-$400

On the Water

Fishing

 Fishing is more than just a popular activity, it's a national obsession. Prize tournaments (see below) draw locals and visitors for a chance at top dollar and the opportunity to show off trophy fish. Catch-and-release is encouraged by local captains and applies to all catches that will not be eaten and all billfish that aren't record contenders. Fly-fishing continues to grow in popularity in these islands. Fly-fishermen should bring all their equipment, however, as guides and charters do not supply saltwater fly rods.

What does all this cost? Prices vary with operator, but here's an idea of what this outdoor adventure will run.

FISHING ADVENTURE COSTS

Deep-sea charters, full day	$450-$1,000
Offshore charters, half-day	$325-$650
Bone, tarpon & reef fishing, full day	$300-$600
(max. 4 anglers, $50 for each add'l person)	
Bone, tarpon & reef fishing, half-day	$200-$400
(max. 4 anglers, $50 for each add'l person)	
Bonefishing guide, half-day *(2 anglers)*	$250

Tipping is traditional. Fishing opportunities found in these islands include:

Shore Fishing

BONEFISH: These three- to eight-pound fish are found in shallow flats and afford any angler a good fight. On Grand Cayman, good bonefishing can be found in the North Sound, South Sound, and Frank Sound areas as well as the coastal flats of South Hole Sound Lagoon. Another hotspot is off Little Cayman and on the southwest coast of Cayman Brac in the shallows. These fish can often be seen mudding in the shallow areas.

Bonefish can be caught all day through, although your success rate depends on many factors, such as weather and tides. Bonefish are on the catch-and-release system.

TARPON: Tarpon up to eight pounds (and up to 15 pounds on Little Cayman), are found on Grand Cayman's North Sound and in Tarpon Pond, a landlocked, mangrove-shaded pond on Little Cayman. Tarpon are also caught above the mosquito-control dykes on Grand Cayman. These fish average three to four pounds. To locate the canals, ask a local resident (and bring along insect repellent – they don't call these mosquito-control dykes for nothing!). Light tackle and saltwater fly rods are preferred for catching these fighting fish. Tarpon are caught on a catch-and-release system.

Adventures

PERMIT: Weighing up to 35 pounds, permit are caught on light tackle in shallow waters. A good fighter, the permit is a cousin of the common pompano, the permit has a jack-shaped body and is found over sandy bottoms.

COMMON POMPANO: Much smaller than the permit, the common pompano averages about eight pounds and is found in schools along Seven Mile Beach as well as on the North Sound side of Barkers. They are caught by the use of bait or artificial lures.

BARRACUDA: This toothy species strikes spoons and can also be caught by fly-fishermen. A good fighter with a strong runs and frequent jumps, the fish is usually found just below the surface.

> **WARNING:** *Barracuda should not be eaten because of ciguatera or tropical fish poisoning. Barracuda consume fish that have dined on algae containing microorganisms that produce toxic substances. The toxin is found in the barracuda and can be deadly.*

Reef Fishing

The many miles of reefs that surround these islands provide a playground for fishermen in search of light tackle action. After chumming to attract the fish, a variety of species can be sought, usually with live bait, such as squid and conch.

GROUPER: The grouper is the largest family of saltwater fish and makes an excellent meal. The Nassau grouper, with mottled coloring, is the most popular in these waters and is usually under three feet in size.

JACK CREVALLE: A tireless fighter, this jack averages five to eight pounds and is often found in large schools.

MUTTON SNAPPER: Another good dining choice, the mutton snapper is brightly colored and has a black spot on each side of its body. Running five to 10 pounds, this fish is often caught with bucktails and plugs.

YELLOWTAIL SNAPPER: This snapper is sought for its tireless fighting, as well as for its tasty flesh. Usually weighing one to one and a half pounds, the fish is often taken while drift fishing near the reef after chumming.

Deep-sea Fishing

Charters seek gamefish, including blue marlin, yellowfin tuna, wahoo, dolphin (dorado) and barracuda, all caught year-round. Strikes occur as close as a quarter-mile from land at the point where the turquoise waters drop into inky darkness and deep water begins. Taking out a charter boat is not an inexpensive proposition, but for many visitors it's the highlight of their trip. The cost of a half-day charter begins at about US $400 and may run as high as $1,000 for a full-day excursion with state-of-the art equipment and tackle.

BLUE MARLIN: This top gamefish is often caught on light tackle while trolling the deep water around the islands. It is a fighter, a favorite with deep-sea fishermen, and can be caught both on artificial lures and with whole bait fish. Blue marlin here don't reach the proportions of those found off some islands (they average 200 pounds or less in the Cayman Islands), but they are caught year-round.

Boats prepare for a deep-sea fishing trip on Grand Cayman.

Adventures

EARTH WATCH: *The government of the Cayman Islands encourages the catch and release of the blue marlin to help maintain numbers in these waters. The government offers free citations to anglers who release their marlin; a request form can be obtained from the boat's captain or the charter boat booking office. Also, captains can point anglers to local taxidermists that make trophy mounts for released fish based on their estimated size.*

DOLPHIN: Not the mammal. This gamefish is noted for its heavy "forehead" and high speed. At 10 to 15 pound each, the blue and yellow dolphin are found near floating debris or patches of seaweed. Drawn to feathers and spoons, the fish also likes bait such as flying fish (its favorite diet), squid, and mullet. Summer is the best time for landing dolphin.

YELLOWFIN TUNA: Summer months especially bring this fighting fish to Cayman anglers. Averaging 30 to 40 pounds, the yellowfin is a powerful swimmer. It is usually caught on heavy line (its size can run much larger than average). The yellowfin is highly sought after and is commonly voted the best tuna for eating. Yellowfin tuna usually are caught during the spring.

BLACKFIN TUNA: This tuna is often caught while drift fishing and is an excellent fighter. Weighing six to eight pounds, the blavkfin is a good eating fish.

SKIPJACK TUNA: This tuna is sometimes caught when trolling for larger tuna. It averages 12 to 15 pounds.

WAHOO: Considered one of the best gamefish because of its fighting ability, the wahoo can obtain a speed of up to 50 mph. This deepwater fish is good for eating, and is a member of the mackerel family. Fish for wahoo from November through March.

Fishing Tournaments

Fishing tournaments are major events in these islands. The largest is the **Million Dollar Month**, held in June. This month-long event attracts anglers from around the world who come to test their skills. The tournament takes place at The Links at SafeHaven. Registration is $200 plus boat charter expenses and is open to amateur and professional anglers. Boat/group registration fees are US $1,000. See *Festivals*, page 32, for details on the prizes and contacts.

The Cayman Islands Angling Club and the Rotary Club also sponsor local fishing tournaments for both residents and visitors. The CI Angling Club holds tournaments in February, March, May, at the end of August and in November.

For information, call Donna Sjostrom at ☎ (345) 949-7099 or fax (345) 949-6819. The **Rotary Club** hosts its tournament in September; for details ☎ (345) 949-5544.

The best source of information about fishing in the Cayman Islands is a 30-page guide published by the Department of Tourism. For a copy of the *Cayman Islands Fishing Guide*, ☎ (345) 949-0623 or stop by the tourist office while in George Town.

If you'd like to meet other anglers, call about attending a meeting of the **Cayman Islands Angling Club** (☎ 345-949-7099); they welcome visitors. Another good way to "talk fish" is to stop in at the **Flying Bridge Bar** at the Indies Suites (☎ 345-945-5025). Tournament fishermen Ronnie and Bunnie Foster hear plenty of tall tales here. You might also consider attending a meeting of the Cayman Islands Angling Club (Box 30280 SMB).

Fishing Operators

The following booking agencies represent independent Caymanian captains who can arrange charter excursions and fishing off the Cayman coasts:

Grand Cayman

Bayside Watersports, Seven Mile Beach
☎ (345) 949-1750
This operator has 10 boats ranging from a 20-foot Seacraft to a 53-foot sportfisherman (max. of eight persons). Deep-sea, bone, tarpon, and reef fishing available.

Black Princess Charters, Seven Mile Beach
☎ (345) 949-0400/3821
A 38-foot boat accommodates up to six fishermen
for deep-sea fishing (full- or half-day) or a half-day
of bone, tarpon and reef fishing.

Charterboat Headquarters, Seven Mile Beach
☎ (345) 945-4340
Nine boats, from 24 to 41 feet, accommodate from
four to eight fishermen for deep-sea and reef
fishing.

Captain Crosby Ebanks' C&G Watersports
Seven Mile Beach
☎ (345) 947-4049
In business for 35 years, this operation offers full-
and half-day deep-sea excursions, as well as bone,
tarpon, and reef fishing.

Deep Sea Fox, George Town
☎ (345) 945-4340
A 40-foot Viking boat accommodates eight
fishermen for a full- or half-day of deep-sea
fishing.

Island Girl Charters, George Town
☎ (345) 947-3029
Island Girl specializes in deep-sea fishing and live
bait, drift fishing for yellowfin tuna and marlin.
Also offers night fishing for snapper and shark.
Charters for six participants are offered on a
28-foot boat.

One Day at a Time, Bodden Town
☎ (345) 947-2244
This 54-foot vessel accommodates 10 persons with
three staterooms, each with private bath, as well
as a fully equipped kitchen, washer and dryer.
Full- and half-day deep-sea fishing trips available.

Peacemaker Charters, Seven Mile Beach
☎ (345) 916-2478
Up to eight persons accommodated on this 48-foot boat for deep-sea and reef fishing.

Sunlight Charters, George Town
☎ (345) 945-4340
Maximum of six fishermen on this 34-foot vessel. With 20 years in operation, Sunlight offers full- and half-day bone, tarpon, and reef fishing.

Temptress, West Bay
☎ (345) 949-0400
A 26-foot Pacemaker accommodates up to four fishermen for a full- or half-day of deep-sea fishing or a half-day of reef fishing.

Cayman Brac

Brac Caribbean Beach Village
☎ (800) 791-7911
Groups up to four can book a full- or half-day of deep-sea, bone, tarpon, and reef fishing.

Capt. Edmund "Munny" Bodden
☎ (345) 948-1228
In operation 38 years, this guide specializes in bone fishing. Up to four fishermen can book a full- or half-day of either deep-sea or bone, tarpon, and reef fishing.

Capt. Frankie Bodden
☎ (345) 949-1428
Located at Divi Tiara Beach Resort, Captain Frankie has been in business 31 years and leads full- or half-day deep-sea fishing trips for up to six persons aboard his 30-foot Phoenix.

Adventures

Shelby Charters
☎ (345) 948-0535
Captain Shelby Scott runs full- and half-day excursions – either deep-sea or reef fishing – for up to eight participants.

Southern Comfort
☎ (345) 948-1314
Captain Lemuel Bodden has offered fishing excursions for 25 years. Full- and half-day deep-sea trips available.

Little Cayman

Sam McCoy's Fishing and Diving Lodge
☎ (800) 626-0496
Deep-sea or reef fish with Sam McCoy or his son, Chip. Ice, bait, and tackle provided. A 32-foot Hatteras takes groups as large as eight.

Southern Cross Club
☎ (345) 948-1099
Three vessels, 16 to 24 feet, take groups of two, three or four deep-sea fishing. Full- and half-day reef fishing also available.

Sailing

Sailing excursions are another popular way to enjoy the islands. Charters, sunset cruises, booze cruises, rollicking "pirate" cruises, and more are offered to entertain vacationers, especially on Grand Cayman. Do it yourselfers will find plenty of smaller watercraft: ocean kayaks, Sunfish, Hobie cats, waverunners, and more on Grand Cayman. Sailors can contact the **Grand Cayman Sailing Club** (Box 30513 SMB, Grand Cayman, BWI; ☎ 345-945-4383 or 947-7913) for more information on sailing programs.

Rental prices vary by location, but expect to pay anywhere from $25 to $100 an hour, depending on type of vessel. Catamaran rentals run about $35-$40 per hour.

Opposite: *Diving with green sea turtles.*
© Wayne Hasson, PT & Co.

Above: *Petting rays at Stingray City,* © Permenter & Bigley

Below: *Blowholes at East End,* © Permenter & Bigley

Above: *Historic home with traditional sand garden*, © Permenter & Bigley

Below: *A scuba boat prepares for a trip off George Town*, © Permenter & Bigley

Above: *Blue iguana at the Botanic Garden*, © Permenter & Bigley
Opposite: *The lure of the deep blue sea*, © PT & Co.
Below: *Rum Point*, © Permenter & Bigley

Above: *Green sea turtle,* © Permenter & Bigley
Opposite: *Seven Mile Beach,* © Permenter & Bigley
Below: *The Woodlands Trail at Grand Cayman's Botanic Garden,* © Permenter & Bigley

BOAT RENTALS

Sailboats are available from these watersports operators on Grand Cayman:

Aqua Delights	☎ (345) 945-4786
Cayman Windsurf	☎ (345) 947-7492
Crosby Ebanks C&G Watersports	☎ (345) 945-4049
Don Foster's Watersports	☎ (800) 83-DIVER

Catamaran rentals also available from the following:

Red Sail Sports	☎ (800) 255-6425
Tourist Information & Services	☎ (345) 949-6598

Yachting

Unlike other Caribbean islands, such as St. Martin, Antigua, and the Virgin Islands, the Cayman Islands do not offer bareboat charters or crewed yachts available. In fact, the islands have only limited yachting facilities. The **Cayman Islands Yacht Club** (P.O. Box 30985, SMB, Grand Cayman, BWI; ☎ 345-945-4322, fax 345-4432) has 152 slips. It offers berthing facilities, fuel, electricity, and water hook-ups for craft up to 70 feet. No laundry, store, restaurant, or other amenities are available at this North Sound marina. The Harbour House Boatyard and Marina (P.O. Box 850 GT, Grand Cayman, BWI; ☎ 345-947-1307, fax 947-6093) provides dockage, a small boat slipway, small and large boat storage, and more. This is a working dockyard. The marina is located on Marina Drive at Prospect Park.

Sailors can contact the **Grand Cayman Sailing Club** (Box 30513 SMB, Grand Cayman, BWI; ☎ 345-945-4383 or 947-7913) for more information on sailing programs.

Adventures

Opposite: *Colorful sponges are a diver's delight.*
© PT & Co.

Windsurfing

Windsurfing operators are found on Seven Mile Beach and on Grand Cayman's East End, the top choice for serious windsurfing aficionados. There are two dedicated windsurfing operators in Grand Cayman. Cayman Windsurf, on the East End at Morritt's Tortuga Club and on Seven Mile Beach at SafeHaven, is a BiC Center; beginners are welcome. Sailboards Caribbean, on Seven Mile Beach, is a Mistral certified school.

WATERSPORTS ADVENTURE COSTS

The following represent average prices for watersports activities (in US dollars):

Windsurfing rentals, per hour	$20-$30
Wave Runner rentals, per half-hour	$35-$60
Sailboat rentals, per hour	$20-$30
Ocean kayak rentals, per hour	$15-$22
Catamaran rentals, per hour	$35
Banana boat rentals, per hour	$35
Glass-bottom boat ride, per trip	$22-$33
Dinner cruises	$45-$68
Day sail cruise	$35-$100

The East End is a top windsurfing area because of its stronger winds. Tradewinds of 15 to 25 knots blow during the winter months, dropping to 10 to 15 knots in the summer.

Windsurfing Rentals

Cayman Windsurf	☎ (345) 947-7492
Don Foster's Watersports	☎ (800) 83-DIVER
Red Sail Sports	☎ (800) 255-6425
Sailboards Caribbean	☎ (345) 949-1068
Tourist Information & Services	☎ (345) 949-6598

Sunset Cruises

Fortunately, you don't have to do all the work on your vacation. Let someone else man the helm and just relax for awhile aboard a sunset cruise. It's a great chance to watch for the "green flash," that peculiar meteorological phenomenon that occurs when the sun falls from a cloudless sky into a calm sea. Watch the horizon as soon as the sun begins to touch the sea and continue to watch for a momentary green flash, one that's often sought but rarely seen.

Sunset & Dinner Cruise Operators

Aqua Delights	☎ (345) 945-4786
Bayside Watersports	☎ (345) 949-1750
Beach Club Watersports	☎ (800) 482-3483
Black Princess Charters	☎ (345) 949-0400
Bob Soto's Diving Ltd.	☎ (800) 262-7686
Cayman Delight Cruises	☎ (345) 949-8111
Crosby Ebanks C & G Watersports	☎ (345) 945-4049
Don Foster's (Subsee) Ltd.	☎ (800) SHOREX-1
Kirk Sea Tours, Ltd.	☎ (345) 949-6986
Ocean Safari	☎ (345) 945-1611
Oh Boy Charters	☎ (345) 949-6341
Peacemaker Charters	☎ (345) 916-2478
Red Sail Sports	☎ (800) 255-6425
Scuba Sensations	☎ (800) 767-0445
Southern Comfort, Cayman Brac	☎ (345) 948-1314
Tourist Information & Services	☎ (345) 949-6598
Wet 'n' Wild Watersports	☎ (345) 949-9180

Water Toys

You'll find plenty of tame water fun in the islands as well, especially at the major resort centers. Waverunners, aqua trikes, viewboards, Sunsearcher floats, banana boat rides, paddle cats, paddleboats, and toys for kids of all ages are available to rent. Look for this fun along Seven Mile Beach on Grand Cayman, and, to a

Adventures

much more limited extent, at Brac Reef Beach Resort on Cayman Brac, and at Little Cayman Beach Resort on Little Cayman.

In the Air

Flying Tours

 During high season (December through April), Island Air offers flightseeing tours of the islands. These are conducted by Seabourne Flightseeing Adventures and cost about $60 for a 30-minute tour. For information, contact **Island Air** at ☎ (345) 949-0241.

Day Trips to Little Cayman & Cayman Brac

When you're ready to see a more secluded side of the Cayman Islands, consider a day trip to Cayman Brac or Little Cayman. The Sister Islands are excellent destinations for serious fishermen and divers and a good way to sample the islands (and perhaps consider them for your next trip).

Flights depart Grand Cayman in the early morning, stopping first on Little Cayman and continuing on to Cayman Brac. Once on the ground, you can rent a vehicle (a jeep on Little Cayman) and enjoy a self-guided tour of the island, birdwatching, scuba diving, snorkeling, or fishing. Guided tours are available on Little Cayman; a special package including air, tour, and lunch is offered through Island Air. With twice-daily service from Grand Cayman, Island Air (Monday through Friday, 9 a.m. to 5 p.m.; ☎ 345-949-5252, fax 345-949-7044) departs on the 45-minute flight at 8 a.m. and 3:50 p.m.; return flights depart at 9:55 a.m. and 5:45 p.m. The day-trip package costs US $105 (US $84 for travelers under 12).

Parasailing

If you're ready to enjoy a bird's-eye view of Grand Cayman, sign up for a parasail ride over Seven Mile Beach. This is the only place in the Cayman Islands where parasailing is offered. Cost is about $45. See the *Seven Mile Beach* section, page 144, for a list of operators.

On Wheels

Bicycling

Bicycling is another fun and generally safe way to see the islands. Each island has bicycles for rent. A favorite with bicyclists is Little Cayman, where nearly every accommodation – whether a B&B, hotel or resort – offers complimentary use of bicycles to its guests. For more on cycling, contact the **Cayman Islands Cycling Association**, Box 456 George Town, Grand Cayman, BWI, ☎ (345) 949-8666. The association has events scheduled throughout the year.

Jeeping

Jeep touring is another option. Open-air jeeps are so ubiquitous they could be considered symbols of the adventurous Cayman lifestyle.

Eco-Travel

Birding

One of the most popular eco-tourism events in these islands is birding. Approximately 200 species of birds make their home on these small islands (50 species are known to breed here), from the magnificent frigate bird, with a seven-foot wingspan, to tiny hummingbirds and Cayman parrots.

Serious birders should consider attending a meeting of the **Cayman Islands Bird Club**. The group meets monthly to discuss seasonal sightings. Call the National Trust at ☎ (345) 949-0121 to check on meeting times.

Another good source of birding information is Rudy Powery of **Rudy's Travellers Tours** (☎ 345-949-3208, fax 345-949-1155). The president of the Bird Club, Powery organizes birding tours around the island.

Each of these islands includes protected sanctuaries and good birding sites. Little Cayman, home of the largest colony of red-footed boobies, is a favorite with serious birders. Guided walks are available on Sundays. The island is home to Patricia Bradley, author of *Birds of the Cayman Islands* (see *Bibliography*), considered the best source of information on the islands' feathered residents.

EARTH WATCH: *Currently, a research study on the endangered Cayman parrots is being conducted by the Grambling Cooperative Wildlife Project. Organized by Grambling State University (Louisiana) and Fundacion para la Protecion de la Flora y la Fauna, Universidad de La Habana (Cuba). The group is studying the five populations of parrots on the islands to determine their conservation needs. For information, contact Dr. James Wiley, ☎ (318) 274-2499.*

National Trust

Much of the conservation efforts on the Cayman Islands is due to the efforts of the National Trust. Founded 1987, the trust is charged with conservation of lands, national features and submarine areas of beauty, historic or environmental importance and the protection of flora and fauna. The National Trust has committees representing each of the eight districts on Grand Cayman and one for Little Cayman and Cayman Brac.

To meet its goals, the work of the trust includes several programs:

◆ **The Land Reserves Program** sets aside nature pre-serves. These important facilities are found throughout the islands and include the Mastic Re-serve, Salina Reserve, Queen Elizabeth II Botanic

Park and the Governor Michael Gore Bird Sanctuary on Grand Cayman; the Brac Parrot Reserve, and the Booby Pond Nature Reserve on Little Cayman.

◆ **The Biodiversity Program**, to encourage expert scientists to visit the islands for their research and to assist in trust projects.

◆ **The Priority Species Program**, to identify local wildlife in need of special protection. These projects have included the Blue Iguana Conservation Program. Volunteers also take a census every three years of the parrot populations on Grand Cayman and Cayman Brac to monitor this bird. Research has also been conducted on the West Indian whistling duck. Other projects include a bat conservation program and an endangered plant program.

To learn more about these efforts, check out the trust's Web site at www.cayman.com.ky/pub/ntrust/ or write **National Trust for the Cayman Islands**, P.O. Box 31116 SMB, Grand Cayman, ☎ (345) 949-0121, fax: (345) 949-7494; E-mail -ntrust@candw.ky. While in George Town, stop by the offices on Courts Road off Eastern Avenue.

One of the largest projects of the National Trust is the Salina Reserve, a 650-acre nature reserve on the North Coast. Although not open to the public, the reserve is an important ecological project that combines wetlands and woodlands and offers nesting sites for parrots, caves with bat roosts, and several acres that are a suitable habitat for the rare blue iguana.

Another major project is the conservation of the Central Mangrove Wetland, a long-term project to preserve the wetland that flows into the North Sound. Fundamental to many natural processes, the wetland filters the ground waters and provides a flow of nutrients into the sound. Those nutrients are essential for the food chain upon which the marine life of the North Sound thrive. About 1,500 acres of this area is currently protected as an Environmental Zone under the Marine Parks Law and now the trust is working to increase the wetland protection with land purchases. The entire wetland spans about 8,500 acres and is still largely undeveloped. This region also provides moisture that later falls in the form of rain over the central and western regions of the island (a rainfall that's 40% greater than seen on the eastern side of the island). This region is the home of many species: West Indian whistling ducks, Grand Cayman parrots, hickatees, agoutis, and marine life.

On Horseback

 Horseback riding is an excellent opportunity both to tour some of the island's quieter sections and to romp along the beach. You'll find two operators on Grand Cayman, one offering personalized tours of the West End, the other with rides through George Town's quieter areas and along South Sound.

Cultural Excursions

National Trust

 Along with its eco-tourism activities, the National Trust is charged with preserving the natural, historic, and maritime history of Cayman through preservation of areas, sites, buildings, structures, and objects of historic or cultural significance. One of the first projects undertaken by the Trust was the conservation of the remains of an original wall of Fort George in downtown George Town (see *Adventures, George Town*, page 104). Other projects have included the Old Savannah Schoolhouse, a typical 1940's one-room Government schoolhouse, the Guard House Park, which recalls the history of Bodden Town, Cayman's first capital, and the East End Lighthouse Park.

The trust has gone on to create walking tour brochures for its most historic districts: West Bay, George Town, and Bodden Town. These brochures (available for $1 from the museum, National Trust, and visitors information booth) introduce visitors to Caymanian architecture and are a wonderful way to learn more about the history that makes these islands special.

The National Trust has also played a major role in the preservation of the Pedro St. James Castle, the oldest structure in the Cayman Islands. For more on this project, check out the *East of George Town* section, page 132.

But it's not just the most important historic structures that have drawn the attention of this group; everyday homes and buildings also earn its respect. The National Trust has an ongoing Historic Buildings and Sites Inventory, a computerized reference list of places of historic and architectural interest built before 1950.

To encourage the public to recognize the value of these historic buildings, the trust has a historic plaque program. Also, it honors private citizens who have made a commitment to maintain, rehabilitate or restore historic buildings and sites with an annual "Award of Distinction for the Preservation of Historic Places."

Guided Tours

Both the history and natural history of the area can be learned aboard a **Silver Thatch Excursion** (☎/fax 345-945-6588). These tours are operated by Geddes Hislop, former Public Education Manager Officer for the National Trust, and his wife, Janet. Hislop worked on the interpretive development of two of the island's top environmental attractions: the Queen Elizabeth II Botanic Park and the Mastic Trail. Six different tours are available, including The Eastern Experience (historic sites from Old Prospect to the Ten Sails Monument in East End); Walk the Mastic Trail; Botanic Park Adventures (two options, including the Historic Route and the Environmental Route); A Walk Back In History (historic walking tour of West Bay, central George Town, visit to Old Prospect, Watler's Cemetery and Old Savannah Schoolhouse); and Birdwatching Excursions to one or more natural wildlife habitats (Governor Michael Gore Bird Sanctuary, Meagre Bay Pond, Botanic Park and Malportas Farm).

Hotel pickup and return, drink, and a snack (sandwich and traditional Caymanian pastries) are included. For information write P.O. Box 344WB, Grand Cayman, ☎/fax (345)945-6588.

BRINGING THE FAMILY TO THE CAYMAN ISLANDS

Bringing the kids along on vacation might seem like an adventure in itself, but in the Cayman Islands it's an easy task.

The island has many family-friendly accommodations (with twice as many condominiums as hotels on Grand Cayman) that make children welcome. Condominium units generally accommodate four to eight people and usually include televisions with VCRs as well as full kitchens – to cut back on dining costs and to satisfy picky eaters.

The low crime rate in the Cayman Islands also makes this a top destination for families. Here's a sampling of activities for family travelers:

◆ Cayman Turtle Farm: Children of all ages delight to the tiny newborn turtles and the massive breeders. Kids enjoy picking up turtles in the special tanks (bring along the camera for this excursion) and school age children find the trip an education.

◆ Snuba: Good for children eight years and older, this tethered scuba experience is a great way to introduce youngsters to the sport of scuba diving.

◆ Scuba resort courses: Children age 12 and up can take a resort course in the swimming poole for an introduction followed by a shallow-water dive.

◆ Glass-bottom boat ride: Families with children of all ages enjoy the *Seaworld Explorer*, a semi-submersible that gives you a peek into the undersea world.

◆ *Atlantis Submarine*: Submerging up to a depth of 100 feet, this submarine is good for children but not recommended for those that might be prone to tantrums or fits in enclosed situations (there's no taking unruly kids out of this attraction).

◆ Jolly Roger pirate ship: Yo ho ho! The kids will love a two-hour cruise aboard this replica of a 17th-century Spanish galleon.

◆ Pirate Cave, Bodden Town: Take a look at indigenous Cayman animals – the agouti and a parrot – before heading down to the cave. Pretend you're a pirate in the damp, dark recesses or on the lookout for pirate treasure.

◆ Watersports on Seven Mile Beach and Rum Point: The youngest kids just enjoying splashing in the gentle surf or digging in the sand; older children can ride the banana boat, try their luck on a windsurfer, or snorkel in the clear waters.

◆ Children's resort programs: The Hyatt Regency Grand Cayman offers Camp Hyatt for kids 3-12 years old. Westin Casuarina Resort has Camp Scallywag for children 4-12.

◆ Cardinal D's Park, George Town: This small zoo gives youngsters a look at the Cayman parrot, blue iguana, agouti, whistling ducks, and turtles. A petting zoo is popular with young visitors.

Any one of these attractions is sure to be a hit.

Adventures

Other Adventures

Although it sometimes seems otherwise, there are land-based sports in the Cayman Islands. On Grand Cayman, golfers can select from two courses, one at the Hyatt Regency and the other at The Links at SafeHaven, both along Seven Mile Beach. Tennis players, cyclists, joggers, runners, and other sports buffs will find companionship and often competitions in the islands.

Sports Organizations

Aviation

Cayman Islands Flying Club
Carl McCoy, President
P.O. Box 1725 GT, Grand Cayman
☎ (345) 949-2891, fax (345) 949-6821

Cricket

Cricket Association
Box 1377
Jimmy Powell
☎ (345) 949-8197, weekdays; ☎ (345) 949-3911 (hm)
Weekend matches held from January through June at the Cricket Oval off Thomas Russell Way.

Cycling

Cayman Islands Cycling Association
Box 456 GT
Peter Larder
☎ (345) 949-8666 (CIBC)
Many events scheduled throughout the year. Check *The Caymanian Compass* on Fridays or call for information.

Golf

The Links at SafeHaven Golf Course
Derek Nash, Golf Pro
P.O. Box 1311 GT, Grand Cayman
☎ (345) 949-5988, fax (345) 949-5457
Tournaments scheduled throughout the year. Call for current list.

Britannia Golf Course at the Hyatt Regency
Robert Cummings, Golf Pro
P.O. Box 1588 GT, Grand Cayman
☎ (345) 949-8020, fax (345) 949-8528
Tournaments scheduled throughout the year. Call for current list.

Olympic Games

Olympic Committee
Box 1529 GT
Bobby Nunes
☎ (345) 949-9142

Rugby

Rugby Club
Box 893 GT
Campbell Law, ☎ (345) 949-9876 (wk)
Bernard Knight, ☎ (345) 949-2039
Matches are played at the South Sound Rugby Club pitch from September through March.

Running

Hash House Harriers (running club)
Box 525 GT
Roger Davies
☎ (345) 949-2001
Meetings every Monday at 5:30, locations TBA.

Adventures

Soccer

Cayman Islands Football (Soccer) Association
Jeff Webb, President
P.O. Box 178 GT
☎ (345) 949-4733/6164
Season runs from September though March with
games played at different locations

Tennis

Tennis Club
Box 1813 GT
Scott Smith
☎ (345) 949-9464

Packing For Adventure

All Cayman visitors need to bring:
- ❑ Proof of citizenship
- ❑ Airline tickets
- ❑ Snorkel, fins, mask
- ❑ Sunscreen, aloe vera gel
- ❑ First aid kit
- ❑ Cameras, flash and film
- ❑ Cooler
- ❑ Driver's license for car rental
- ❑ Swimsuit (we usually take two each)
- ❑ All prescriptions (in original bottles)
- ❑ Mini-address book

A four-night stay:

For him
- ❑ 1 pair casual slacks; 1 pair nice slacks or khakis
- ❑ 2 t-shirts; 2 polo or short-sleeve shirts
- ❑ 2 pair of shorts
- ❑ 2 swimsuits

- ❏ 1 pair walking shoes, socks
- ❏ 1 pair sandals or tennis shoes

For her
- ❏ 1 pair casual slacks; 1 casual skirt or 1 dress
- ❏ 1 t-shirt; 2 short-sleeve or sleeveless blouses
- ❏ 2 pair of shorts
- ❏ 2 swimsuits
- ❏ 1 pair walking sandals; 1 pair evening sandals
- ❏ 1 swimsuit cover-up

Divers:
- ❏ "C" card
- ❏ Compass
- ❏ Dive tables
- ❏ Dive computer
- ❏ Weight belt
- ❏ Mesh bag
- ❏ Dive boots
- ❏ Dive skin or light wetsuit
- ❏ Dive light and Cylume sticks
- ❏ Batteries
- ❏ Logbook
- ❏ Emergency medical information
- ❏ Proof of insurance/DAN membership card

Bonefish anglers:
- ❏ Polarized sunglasses
- ❏ Camera to record your catch
- ❏ Wading shoes or boating shoes

Fly-fishing anglers:
- ❏ Bring all equipment; only basic tackle available
- ❏ Camera to record your catch

Boat fishing anglers:
- ❏ Non-skid shoes
- ❏ Camera to record your catch

Adventures

Hikers:
- ☐ Hiking shoes (broken-in)
- ☐ Extra socks
- ☐ Compass
- ☐ Insect repellent

Birders:
- ☐ Binoculars
- ☐ Bird list
- ☐ Copy of *Birds of the Cayman Islands* or your favorite guide

Grand Cayman

George Town

Introduction

For most vacationers, a visit to **George Town** marks the beginning and end of their stay. This capital city is home of both the international airport and the cruise terminal, so a majority of the 1.3 million visitors spend at least some time here.

Cruise ship terminal/waterfront area.

The capital is the social and economic hub of the islands, home to over half the 30,000 residents of Grand Cayman and the base for most of the business and government activity. Don't look for a bustling city, however; George Town is still very much an island community where you'll feel at home strolling the streets, eating at a seaside diner, and enjoying watersports just as you would in the resort areas of Seven Mile Beach.

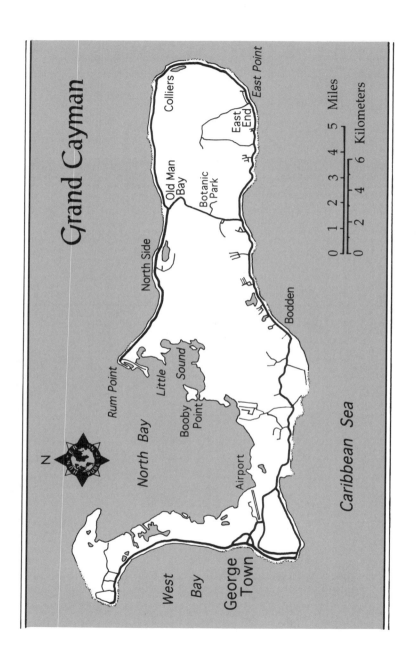

Once, this community was known as The Hogstyes. Today it's a major financial center that ranks right up there with Zurich and Tokyo. Modern, clean, and efficient, this capital city hasn't forgotten its historic roots, however. Just off Hog Sty Bay, historic homes, churches, and other structures are now part of a self-guided walking tour designed by the National Trust.

Much of the activity in George Town takes place along North and South Church Streets, which run parallel to the shoreline. These roads face out to George Town Harbour and are lined with duty-free shops, restaurants, and tourist-oriented businesses. The traffic light where South Church Street forks right onto Shedden Road or continues onto North Church Street (an intersection located by the cruise terminal), is the heart of town.

East of the shoreline, government buildings and banking centers carry on the work of the Cayman Islands, helping the nation hold its spot as one of the monetary centers in the world. Further east, the airport is located on the edge of North South, the shallow body of water that divides George Town, Seven Mile Beach, and the West End from the less developed East End of the island.

South of town, South Church Street winds it way through elegant residential districts, lined with beautiful seaside homes and a few quiet businesses.

Getting Around

Upon arrival at the **Owen Roberts International Airport**, continue through the airport past baggage and outside to the pick-up area. Here, vans and mini-buses offer passenger service to local hotels for a fixed fee.

Hotels in the Cayman Islands are not allowed to send a courtesy van for airport pickup so be prepared to pay for a ride or rent a car.

Transportation around George Town and throughout Grand Cayman is easy. Take your pick from taxis and group vans as well as rental cars, jeeps, bicycles, and scooters.

TAXI CHART

Fares from Owen Roberts International Airport to:

Sunset House	$12
Enterprise B&B	$15
Smith's Cove	$13

Car Rental

Renting a vehicle for at least part of your stay is often the easiest and most economical way to get around, especially if you plan to explore. Car rentals begin at about US $30 per day.

A temporary driver's license is required; you can obtain this from the rental agency by presenting your valid driver's license and paying the US $7.50 fee. You must be 21 or over to rent a vehicle, 25 at agencies. Insurance policies of some rental agencies do not cover drivers under 25.

Remember that driving is on the **left** side throughout the Cayman Islands. Most vehicles are right-hand drive; most 4x4s have a left-hand stick shift.

For a complete listing of rental car companies throughout the islands, see page 40.

On Foot

With the low crime rate in the Cayman Islands, travel on foot is fun and safe. Walking is the easiest way to get around George Town, especially along the waterfront area. Remember, however, to look right when crossing the street.

Guided Tours

Guided tours are an excellent way for first-time visitors to get a good overview. Guided tours are available from most taxi drivers for about US $37.50 for four persons per hour; you can also check with your hotel tour desk for possibilities. Here are several tour operators that offer varying packages:

Burton's Tours
☎ (345) 949-7222, fax (345) 947-6222
Burton Ebanks is a local resident with extensive knowledge of the entire region. He does both group and private tours and we can highly recommend him for his complete knowledge of Grand Cayman.

Elite Limousine Service
☎ (345) 947-2561, fax (345) 949-3834
Elite does sightseeing tours as well as airport transfers.

Evco Tours
☎ (345) 949-2118, fax (345) 949-0137
Sightseeing tours, dinner cruises, cruise ship tours, charter fishing trips, and more.

Majestic Tours
☎ (345) 949-7773, fax (345) 949-8647
Tours and airport transfers.

McCurley's Tours
☎ (345) 947-9626
Sightseeing tours as well as transfers available.

Reids Premier Tours
☎ (345) 949-6531, fax (949) 949-4770
Sightseeing tours, shopping tours, fishing trips, snorkel trips, and more.

Rudy's Travellers Transport, West Bay
☎ (345) 949-3208, fax (345) 949-1155
Rudy Powery, president of the Bird Club, leads guided birding tours as well as sightseeing trips.

Silver Thatch Excursions
☎/fax (345) 945-6588
Cultural and natural history of the area. George Town tours include A Walk Back In History, a walking tour to the region's most historic sites. Birding and nature tours also available. Hotel pickup and return, drink, and a snack (sandwich and traditional Caymanian pastries) are included.

Tropicana Tours Ltd.
☎ (345) 949-0944, fax (345) 949-4507
Sightseeing and watersports.

Vernon's Sightseeing Tours
☎ (345) 949-1509, fax (345) 949-0213
Sightseeing tours, dinner transfers, shopping tours, fishing trips and more offered.

Adventures

On Foot

 Slip on a pair of comfortable shoes and take off on a walking tour of George Town. A brochure produced by the National Trust covers a self-guided walking tour of about two hours in length; copies of *An Historical Walking Tour, Central George Town* are available from the National Trust, at the tourism office, and at the National Museum for $1.

The tour begins at the cruise ship landing and includes the site of **Fort George**, built around 1790 to defend the island from Spanish invasions. The fort site is located at the intersection of Harbour Drive and Fort Street.

Nearby, the **Seamen's Memorial** remembers the 153 Caymanians lost at sea. Across the street the **Elmslie Memorial Church** was built by shipwright Captain Rayal Bodden; inside the ceiling is constructed to resemble a schooner's hull. The adjacent cemetery has grave markers that resemble houses, a typical style seen at the island's cemeteries.

Other stops on the walking tour include the **Legislative Assembly Building**, **the post office**, and walk-bys of **traditional houses** with Caymanian sand gardens.

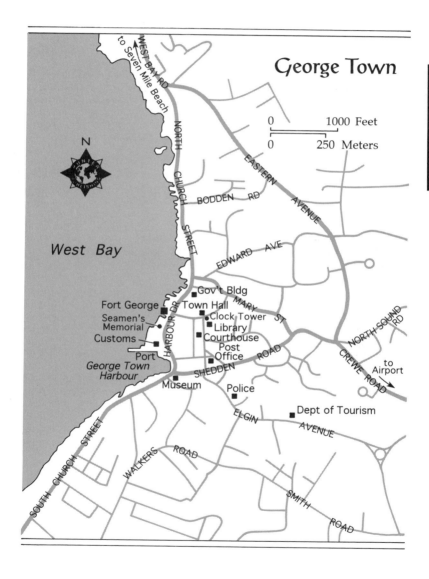

Underwater

Scuba Diving

 Although George Town may be the capital city, it is by no means just a business center: here it's just as appropriate to don a mask and tank as a three piece suit. The waters off George Town are protected as a marine park and boast numerous dive sites. Two major dive operations, **Eden Rock Dive Shop** on South Church Road, ☎ (345) 949-7243, and **Parrot's Landing**, ☎ (345) 949-7884, provide instruction and equipment. You'll find many good sites off the George Town coast:

Scuba divers at Eden Rock.

Eden Rock and Devil's Grotto: Eden Rock Dive Shop on South Church Road is the entry point for one of George Town's most popular dive sites. Eden Rock and the Devil's Grotto, located about 150 yards from the shore, are shallow dives but unique. Both are a labyrinth of grottos running out from the shore. Eden Rock is popular not only with divers but also with snorkelers who enjoy the easy entrance and a view of the tunnels and often large tarpon. Eden Rock and Devil's Grotto have a depth of 30-50 feet.

Parrot's Reef: Parrot's Reef and, beyond that, Sunset Reef, are dive sites filled with marine life. They are just yards from shore. Parrot's Reef has a depth of 30-60 feet.

Japanese Gardens: Located off the reef at South Sound, just east of George Town, this dive lies 30 to 60 feet below the surface and is often recommended for beginning divers. Like a little bonsai forest, the area is dotted with staghorn corals and is a good site for underwater photographers. Includes some swim-throughs.

The Wreck of the *Balboa*: The hurricane of 1932 accounted for the wreck of this freighter, which today lies 25 to 40 feet below the surface. Some of the ship remains intact, but other parts were blown away to clear the traffic channel. This is a popular night dive because of the depth (and because, during daytime hours, this site sits right in the George Town Harbour waterway). Rich with marine life from corals to sponges to brilliant parrotfish, this is one of Grand Cayman's top dive sites.

The Black Forest: Beautiful black coral and waving gorgonians make this site indeed seem like the Black Forest. Located at 60 to 100 feet, this wall dive is just off the South West Point, but isn't accessible as a shore dive.

Smiths Cove: Although often considered a snorkel site, Smiths Cove on South Church Street just south of George Town is an easy shore dive as well. The reef starts just a few feet from the surface and divers can also explore the West Wall from this location.

Smiths Cove, a popular snorkel and dive site.

Wreck of the *Cali*: Located in just over 20 feet of water about 100 feet offshore, save the *Cali* for your departure day when you can't scuba dive. (It's a shallow dive for beginners.) The *Cali* offers a great snorkel experience and is a good way to finish off your Cayman vacation.

Snorkeling

Snorkelers will find a good spot just south of **Smiths Cove Park**, along South Church Street. This free park has good snorkeling along the rocks on its north side; covered picnic tables and plenty of shade make it a popular lunch site. **Eden Rock** is also frequented by snorkelers. Another favorite is **Soto's Reef**, sometimes called Passion Reef, located behind Soto's Dive Shop (below the Lobster Pot restaurant on North Church Street). One of the top snorkel destinations is the wreck of the *Cali*. Located a short swim from Calico Jack's in just 20 feet of water, this wreck is a good opportunity for snorkelers to view a wreck site, an experience usually reserved for advanced scuba divers.

Underwater Photography

The best way to bring home memories of a Cayman dive is with underwater photography. If you're interested in learning the skills needed to produce good underwater shots, consider a half-day or a week-long course taught by Cathy Church, who was named best underwater photo pro by the readers of Rodale's *Scuba Diving* magazine. Church offers private instruction and use of underwater video and 35mm equipment. Cathy Church's Underwater Photo Centre and Galleries also offers E6 film processing, underwater camera rentals, and Nikonos repair. Open daily at Sunset House Hotel. For information, ☎ (345) 949-7415.

Tethered Scuba Diving

If you're new to underwater adventure, an excellent way to sample the sport of scuba diving is with snuba. This unique adventure combines snorkeling and scuba diving to give even non-swimmers an opportunity to explore life below the surface. Anyone eight years or older can enjoy this safe activity, which can be experienced by handicapped and senior vacationers as well.

The equipment utilized by snuba participants is much like that used by certified scuba divers. Visitors don a weight belt to help achieve neutral buoyancy then add mask, fins, and a snorkel.

Regulators are assigned and usually two swimmers share an air tank, which floats on the surface in an inflatable raft pulled by the snuba instructor. Twenty-foot-long tubes connect snuba divers to this air tank. Up to six swimmers can enjoy this experience with each snuba instructor.

The experience is similar to a shallow-water dive but without the weight of an air tank on your back. After a short safety and usage course (about 10 to 15 minutes), snuba divers swim out from shore and enjoy the spectacle of marine life found just yards away. Five-foot-long tarpon are often spotted (every evening the nearby restaurants feed these silvery beggars) as well as crabs and parrot-fish.

The highlight of the snuba experience is the chance to dive the wreck of the *Cali*, a four-masted schooner. Originally wrecked on the reef, the Great Hurricane of 1932 washed the ruins closer to shore, creating one of the Caribbean's shallowest wreck dives. Snuba participants get within feet of the iron wreckage, which is now home to a variety of marine life.

Snuba instructor Mark Regal is one of the top watersports operators we've met in the Caribbean. His instruction is top notch and easy for beginners to understand; his attention to safety is thorough without instilling fear. Mark has taken down non-swimmers, towing them on a rope.

Ticket prices are US $65 per person. Dives are scheduled at 8:30, 10, 11:30, 1, and 2:30 daily. For more information, write **Divers Supply**, P.O. Box 1995, George Town, Cayman Islands, BWI or ☎ (345) 949-4373.

Another tethered scuba operation we have not had the opportunity to try is **Cayman Glide Divers Ltd**. This operator uses Diveman, a product that straps an air reservoir and pump unit to the diver. Cables connect from the unit to the diver's legs and a kick makes the pump draw fresh air from a 20-foot tube connected to the surface. This fills the reservoir for several breaths. The unit requires less than 30 minutes of training, then participants rent equipment. An introductory course is $20; a half-day gear rental is $30, full days run $50. For more information, contact Cayman Glide Divers Ltd. (P.O. Box 2488 GT, Grand Cayman), ☎ (345) 945-2711 or fax: (345) 945-2711.

Grand Cayman

Submarines

Atlantis Submarine, Harbour Dr., ☎ (800) 887-8571, (800) 253-0493 or (345) 949-7700. If you're curious about what lies below the water's surface, the 48-passenger *Atlantis* is the perfect way to have a peek at Grand Cayman's underwater world. Swimmers and non-swimmers alike enjoy safe, air-conditioned, comfortable travel to 100 feet below the surface aboard the *Atlantis* with a narrated view of coral gardens, sponge gardens, the undersea wall, and more.

The Atlantis Submarine.

Visitors buy tickets at the headquarters located just south of the cruise ship terminal on Harbour Drive in downtown George Town. Tours operate six days a week. The dive takes 50 minutes, but the total tour time is 1 hour and 40 minutes. You'll board an open-air boat and travel out to the dive site just off George Town's shore. Bench seating runs the length of the sub and all visitors have a porthole from which to enjoy the underwater scene.

After viewing the marine life, don't be surprised to see some human life forms approaching the submarine – these are the Atlantis divers. Wearing armored wetsuits to protect against fish nibbles, these divers feed clouds of hungry fish and provide good photo opportunities.

Bring along your camera on this fascinating tour, but load film with an ASA rating of 1000. Your flash is useless in the confines of the sub because it will reflect off the portholes. The ASA 1000 film is fast enough to capture the colorful images you'll witness without using a flash.

Ticket prices are $72 per person; children under 12 are half price. No children under three feet tall are permitted.

Atlantis Submarine Submersible, Harbour Drive, ☎ (800) 887-8571, (800) 253-0493 or (345) 949-7700. Another option is a ride on an *Atlantis Research Submersible*, also operating from the Atlantis office on Harbour Drive. Plunging down to a depth of up to 1,000 feet below the surface, this research vessel offers a one-of-a-kind experience. The 22-foot sub carries two passengers and a pilot and is the only sub of its type available to the public. Several times a day, the yellow vessel plunges down the Cayman Wall to depths far beyond the range of sports scuba divers.

The vessel has a large, three-foot-diameter convex window and the two passengers sit side by side in front of this viewport. The view varies with the depth: from 200 to 400 feet below the surface are colorful sponges and corals in what's termed the "sponge belt." Hundreds of sponges blanket the vertical wall in forms ranging from 20-foot-long orange rope sponges to gigantic barrel sponges. From 650 to 1,000 feet, living formations give way to limestone pinnacles that house deep-sea creatures, such as stalked crinoids, porcelain corals and glass sponges. Termed the "haystack" zone, the haystacks or limestone blocks stand over 150 feet tall. Here, light no longer penetrates the sea and the research sub illuminates the inky blackness with powerful lights.

The highlight of many trips is a visit to the *Kirk Pride*, a shipwreck that sits on a ledge at 800 feet. This 180-foot freighter sank in a storm in 1976 and its fate was unknown until the wreck was discovered by an *Atlantis Research Submarine* in 1985.

As with the *Atlantis Submarine* trip, bring along your camera for this excursion; load ASA 1000 film so you will not need a flash. The tour last about an hour.

Tickets are US $295-395 per person (depending on type of dive). Five dives are scheduled Monday through Friday. Advance reservations are strongly recommended.

On the Water

 Seaworld Explorer, South Church St., ☎ (345) 949-8534. Not a true submarine but actually a glorified glass-bottom boat, the *Seaworld Explorer* sits next to *Atlantis Submarine* (see *Underwater*, below) on South Church Street. The *Seaworld Explorer* is a good option for those who might feel a little claustrophobic about a submarine adventure (since it does not actually submerge). Visitors descend into a glass observatory and view marine life as well as two shipwrecks. The Explorer travels to the *Cali*, a schooner that hit the reef in 1944, and the *Balboa*, a freighter from Cuba destroyed by a hurricane. Today, the wrecks are encased in corals and filled with fish life. Tickets for the *Seaworld Explorer* are US $33 per person; children 2-12 are US $19. Tours last one hour.

Jolly Roger, ☎ (345) 949-8534. Yo ho ho, the pirate ship anchored off George Town's shores is friendly and lots of fun. The *Jolly Roger*, which claims to be the only authentic replica of a 17th-century Spanish galleon in the Caribbean, offers several kinds of buccaneering fun. On Wednesday, Thursday, and Friday, take a pirate cruise (walk the plank if you don't set the sails!) where you can fire the cannon and witness a sword fight. Saturday brings a champagne breakfast cruise. Dinner cruises and sunset sails also offered (see *Nightlife*, below). Prices are US $29 for the pirate cruise, $25 for the breakfast cruise. Tours depart from Bayside in George Town Harbour.

In the Air

 Aerial tours of Grand Cayman are available through Island Air with **Seaborne Flightseeing Adventures**. The 25-minute tour includes a look at Grand Cayman from a 19-passenger Twin Otter aircraft. Tours are scheduled only from December through June. Cost is US $56. For information or reservations, ☎ (345) 949-6029. **Cayman Helicopters Ltd.** (☎ 345-949-4400) also offers a flightseeing tour aboard a six-passenger vehicle.

Sightseeing

Cayman Islands National Museum, Harbour Drive, ☎ (345) 949-8368. The best way to learn more about Cayman history and culture is to stop by this museum, just across from the cruise ship terminals. It is housed in the Old Courts Building, one of the few 19th-century structures left on the island. Outdoor steps lead up to the second story of the building and those 12 steps gave rise to a Cayman saying: "walking the 12 steps," which meant you were being taken to court. Over the years, this seaside building has served as a courthouse, jail, and meeting hall, and today it houses over 2,000 artifacts that recall the history of these islands. Created in 1979 by a museum law and opened in 1990, the museum collects items of historic, scientific, and artistic relevance.

Cayman Islands National Museum.

Visitors enter on the ground floor. Starting with an eight-minute slide show about the history of the islands, they then enjoy a self-guided tour of the museum, with displays on all facets of Caymanian life. A bathymetric map displays the depth of the seas around the Cayman Islands, including the Cayman Trench at 23,750 feet below sea level. Other exhibits recall facets of natural history: mangrove swamps which create a rich birding environment; Caymanite, a semi-precious stone unique to the Cayman Islands; and displays on local marine life.

Some of the most fascinating displays recall the early economy of the Caymanians. An oral history program captures the history of the early turtlers who made a living capturing the now protected reptiles. Exhibits show the tools of the early residents, including: the muntle, a club used to kill fish when they were caught; the calabash, a versatile gourd that, once dried, had many uses; sisal switches used to beat mosquitoes away; and wompers, sandals worn on the East End, originally made from leather and later from old tires.

After your museum tour, you'll exit through the museum shop, a good source of Caymanian-made items. The shop, housed in the old jail with part of the old coral stone wall still exposed, has a good selection of books and maps of the Cayman Islands. (If you don't have time for a museum tour, you can enter through the store for a little shopping.)

Admission is CI $4 for adults, CI $2 for children and seniors. The museum is open Monday through Friday 9:30 a.m. to 5:30 p.m., Saturday 10 a.m. to 4 p.m.

EARTH WATCH: *Those interested in Caymanian history can join the museum for as little as $10. Membership includes unlimited admission, invitations to members-only previews and receptions, 10% discount in the museum shop, newsletter on events and exhibits, and volunteer opportunities. Members also have access to the museum library by appointment. For membership information, ☎ (345) 949-8368 or fax (345) 949-0309.*

Post Office, Edward St. and Cardinal Ave., ☎ (345) 949-7001. A great spot to mingle with local residents is the main post office in George Town, located between the Royal Bank of Canada and the Bank of Nova Scotia. Grand Cayman has no postal delivery routes, so all mail is placed in the boxes of this open-air post office. Stop by the philatelic bureau – open 8:30 to 5:30 Monday through Friday and 8:30 to 1 on Saturday – for Caymanian stamps and first day covers.

Stingray Brewery, Red Bay Rd., ☎ (345) 947-6699. A new attraction east of town is the Stingray Brewery. This microbrewery produces a local wheat beer that's sold throughout the island in stores, restaurants, and bars. The brewery is closed on Sundays.

Cardinal D's Park, off Courts Rd., ☎ (345) 949-8855. This small zoo is a good stop for families. Over 60 species of exotic birds, including Cayman parrots, whistling ducks, agoutis, blue iguanas, turtles, miniature ponies, emus, and more are on display. A petting zoo and snack bar make this attraction popular with kids. Open daily; guided tours available at 11 and 2.

Where to Stay

Hotels & Resorts

Sunset House Resort, ☎ (800) 854-4767, (345) 949-7111; fax (345) 949-7101. $-$$. Located just south of George Town, Sunset House is a favorite with divers. Just offshore lie both the reef and several shipwrecks, making this a virtual playground for those interested in underwater adventure.

There's nothing fancy about Sunset House – it's designed for those whose vacation is the portion spent in the water, not necessarily on land. Guest rooms include standard accommodations overlooking the courtyard and deluxe rooms with ocean or garden views. Two suites are also available.

Divers and those who want to learn can utilize the full-service dive operation, which offers resort courses, certification courses, check-out dives, and advanced instruction. When you're suited up and ready to go, it's just a matter of stepping off the shore ladder and into the aqua-playground. For more distant dives, six custom dive boats take divers on two-tank dives around the island while *Manta*, a catamaran, takes experienced divers on all-day, three-tank dives.

Facilities at this 59-room resort include a restaurant featuring local and continental cuisine, gift shop, oceanfront bar, freshwater swimming pool and hot tub, full-service dive shop, six dive boats, and the Sunset Underwater Photo Centre, which offers half-day to week-long courses.

Condos & Small Inns

Ambassadors Inn, ☎ (800) 648-7748, (345) 949-7577; fax (345) 949-7050. $. Located near Smiths Cove one mile south of George Town, this small property is ideal for those on a budget. With just 18 guest rooms, the atmosphere is cozy and friendly. Rooms include air-conditioning, ceiling fans, private bath, telephone, cable TV, and daily maid service. Divers will be happy to note there's a dive shop; Ambassador Divers offers packages for guests that include daily boat dives and unlimited shore dives. The inn also has a restaurant, auto and moped rental agency, and bicycle rentals.

Dive packages are available for $396 (single occupancy) for three nights in high season; $363 in low season. A bed-and-breakfast plan is also available.

Guest Houses

Enterprise Bed and Breakfast, ☎ (345) 947-6009; fax (345) 716-8380. $. Located on Red Bay, this bed and breakfast carries the theme of – you guessed it – Star Trek. Rooms include a double and a twin bed (one room has a queen bed), air-conditioning, private bath, TV, microwave, small refrigerator, bar sink, dining table and chairs, and a patio or balcony. Facilities include a freshwater rinse station for scuba gear.

For reservations, contact the booking office at ☎ (818) 716-8380 or fax (818) 348-0433; mailing address for reservations is 5160 Llano Drive #I, Woodland Hills, CA 91364. Credit cards are not accepted; smoking is not permitted.

Erma Eldemire's Guest House, ☎ (800) 405-2187, (345) 949-5387; fax (345) 949-6987. $. Located one mile south of George Town, this guest house is a 10-minute walk from Smith Cove.

Rooms include private bath, air-conditioning, and ceiling fan. Guests have access to a refrigerator and hot plate (studios and the one apartment have private kitchen facilities). Daily maid service, except on Sunday. Winter rates begin at US $65 for single and $70 for double occupancy, $80 for a studio apartment, and $100 for a one-bedroom apartment; summer rates start at $55. Credit cards and checks are not accepted. A three-day deposit is required with reservation.

Where to Eat

American

Blue Parrot, South Church St. at Coconut Harbour, ☎ (345) 949-9094. $-$$. Not necessarily the place to go for a quiet dinner, this restaurant boasts the island's largest TV screen. Order up grilled seafood, sandwiches, and salads for lunch and dinner.

Calico Jack's, North Church St., ☎ (345) 949-4373. $$. Dine under the light of the stars at this fun eatery located behind Calico Jack's Pirate Emporium. A weekly barbecue serves up chicken and all the fixin's; burgers are also a favorite. The nightly tarpon feeding is a good reason to stay a little longer.

Bars/Pubs

Hog Sty Bay Café and Pub, North Church Street at Mary Street, ☎ (345) 949-6163. $. Order up a half-pint of Tennent's Extra or Stone's Best Bitter at this bar that calls itself the best British pub for 5,000 miles. Along with an extensive beer selection and pub grub, the place keeps hopping with English Premier League football on weekends, darts on Monday and Wednesday, British comedies on the telly, and live music many nights. Pub menu includes steak and kidney pie, cod and chips, chicken and mushroom pie, bangers and mash, and shepherd's pie. Out on the patio, enjoy a menu featuring local seafood.

Ports Of Call Beach Bar, at The Wharf on West Bay Rd., ☎ (345) 949-2231. Located right on the water's edge, the open-air bar boasts an uninterrupted view of the setting sun. A school of huge tarpon usually lingers below the deck, waiting for scheduled handouts, and live music is offered most evenings.

Caribbean

Billy's Place, North Church Street, ☎ (345) 949-0470. $. Sample local favorites, such as fish Cayman style, jerk conch, conch stew, jerk pork, curry chicken, curry goat, ox tail, and stew beans, at this inexpensive eatery. Start with Samosa, an appetizer of flaky pastry stuffed with peas and potatoes and served with mint and mango chutney. Jerk burgers, jerk pizza, and Indian favorites, such as curry shrimp and chicken tikka (marinated chicken baked in a clay oven), round out the menu. Open for lunch and dinner Monday through Saturday; dinner only on Sundays.

Italian

Casanova Ristorante, Old Fort Building, ☎ (345) 949-7633. $$$. Specializing in romantic dining, this restaurant is decorated with Italian artwork. An extensive menu offers penne pasta sautéed with Caribbean lobster, linguine with clams, potato dumplings with homemade pesto sauce, veal piccata, and many seafood dishes. Open for lunch Monday through Saturday; dinner nightly. Reservations suggested.

Seafood

Crow's Nest, South Church Street, ☎ (345) 949-936. $$-$$$. West Indian favorites fill the menu here. Start with conch fritters or a jerk chicken sampler and then enjoy red bean soup or conch chowder. Entrées include Jamaican chicken curry, turtle farm steak topped with a peppery cream vermouth sauce, and red snapper, mahi mahi, mako shark, or swordfish prepared grilled, pan-fried, or blackened. Open for lunch Monday through Saturday, dinner daily.

Hog Sty Bay Café and Pub, North Church Street at Mary Street, ☎ (345) 949-6163. $$-$$$. Dine indoors or out on the seaside patio and this relaxed and fun café. Located within the pub (see above), the restaurant serves up a mix of seafood and steaks, as well as salads and soups. Most appetizers and entrées are prepared with an island flair, such as conch fritters, a red conch chowder that's a meal in itself, pan-fried red snapper, seafood pasta from hell (shrimp, scallops, lobster and fish in a hot and spicy citrus sauce), and favorites like coconut shrimp. Make reservations for seats on the patio, a great place to enjoy sunset.

Island Taste Restaurant and Lounge, Church Street, ☎ (345) 949-4945. $$. This open-air, second-floor restaurant is set across the street from the *Atlantis Submarine* office. Specializing in tropical and Mediterranean cuisine, the menu includes a wide variety of pasta dishes as well as lobster tail, conch steak, dolphin, snapper, and a daily captain's catch. Save room for the key lime pie. Open for lunch and dinner.

Lobster Pot, North Church Street. ☎ (345) 949-2736. $$$-$$$$. This second-floor restaurant, built with a view of the George Town Harbour, serves up seafood accompanied by an extensive wine list. Lobster and surf and turf are favorites, as well as grilled salmon filet, mango chicken, Cayman turtle steak, seafood curry, and cracked conch. Save this one for a special night out; prices are high, even by Cayman standards.

The Wharf, West Bay Rd., ☎ (345) 949-2231. $$$. Just past George Town at the start of the beach, The Wharf is a favorite with couples. This seaside restaurant and bar is open for lunch on weekdays and dinner nightly, featuring continental and Caribbean cuisine. Located right on the water's edge, the open-air bar offers an uninterrupted view of the setting sun. A school of huge tarpon waits below the deck, waiting for scheduled handouts, and live music is offered most evenings.

Shopping

George Town is the best place to shop in the Cayman Islands. Here, you'll find a good selection of duty-free china, perfumes, leather goods, watches, crystal, and more. Jewelry (mostly gold) is a popular buy and available at stores such as 24 K-Mon Jewellers (Treasure Island Resort), Savoy Jewellers (Fort St. and Church St.), and The Jewelry Center (also on Fort Street). For china and crystal, check out the Kirk Freeport Centre (Albert Panton St.). Know your prices before you leave home, however; those "bargains" may or may not be such a good buy. Some of the really good deals are on

Cayman-made items. **Caymanite**, a stone found only on the eastern edge of Grand Cayman's East End and the bluff on Cayman Brac, is sold throughout the islands mounted as jewelry. The semi-precious stone, a form of dolomite, ranges from a light beige to a beautiful amber color and is often mounted in a gold setting. Another popular island purchase is the **Tortuga Rum Cake** (☎ 800-444-0625), made using five-year-old Tortuga Gold Rum. Sealed in a red tin, the cake is the product of a 100-year-old family recipe. If you want to skip the cake, take home a bottle of Tortuga, Blackbear, or Cayman Gold Rum. **Black coral jewelry** is also a widespread commodity, but note that its harvesting depletes the sea's black coral supply. Only jewelers licensed to remove the coral may do so. Without a certificate testifying that your purchase is from an approved seller, your black coral may be confiscated in Customs. Anything made with turtle products should also be avoided. All goods – including oils, steaks, shells, and jewelry – made from turtles and turtle shells have been banned by US Customs. Even passengers traveling through the US to other nations will have to surrender turtle products at US Customs. Locals products you won't have to worry about clearing through Customs are arts and crafts. Look for **birdhouses** made from coconuts, **brooms** woven from thatch, and **pepper sauce** distilled form fiery scotch bonnet peppers to capture the spirit of the islands.

Nightlife

Sunset sails are a good way to end the day and are offered by numerous operators (many with complimentary hotel pick-up). A unique place to watch for the green flash is aboard the *Jolly Roger*. Sunset cruises are offered on Tuesday, Thursday, Saturday, and Sunday. Other nights, a dinner cruise starts with rum punch and features a Cayman-style dinner. Sunset sails are US $25 per person; dinner cruises run $54. ☎ (345) 949-8534 for reservations. Tours depart from Bayside in George Town Harbour.

Tarpon feeding from George Town Harbour restaurants is another popular evening event. Calico Jack's and The Wharf both schedule tarpon feeding, when the waters churn with these large silvery marine creatures hungrily snatching up chunks of fish.

East of George Town

Introduction

For all the glitz of Seven Mile Beach and the high finance of George Town, the land east of the capital city is simple and countrified, charming visitors with a true Caribbean atmosphere. Condos are few and far between, sandwiched instead by miles of unimproved land and small Caymanian cottages. Cattle graze in the fields, beaches stretch for miles without a watersports operator in sight.

Rum Point.

East of George Town lies the bulk of Grand Cayman. A single road leads east of town along the South Sound to the communities of **Spotts**, **Bodden Town** (the original capital city of the Cayman Islands), and miles of land unchanged by progress. This main highway changes names continually – it's called Jackson Road, Poinciana Road, Shamrock Drive, Church Street, Eastern Highway, A2, A3, A4, and more. Just stay on the main road and continue east; you won't get lost.

This main road winds past several good swimming areas, including a public beach in **Spotts** and another in **Breakers**. Just past

Breakers, you'll have a choice: continue east to the easternmost portion of the island, or turn north. If you turn north on Frank Sound Road, you'll pass the **Mastic Trail** and the **Queen Elizabeth Botanic Park**, both excellent attractions for those interested in the flora and fauna of the island. The road continues to Old Man Bay and meets up with the main road along the northern stretch of the island.

If you don't turn north on Frank Sound Road, you can follow the main road alongside some of the most rugged shoreline on Grand Cayman. Just before the road begins its northern turn on the easternmost stretch of the island, it passes an attraction called the **Blowholes**, where the sea spews forth between the rocks with each wave. Continuing east toward the sea you'll see the sites of two of the island's most famous shipwrecks: The Wreck of the Ten Sails (1794) and the *Cumberland Transport* (1767). Turning north, the road continues past a largely undeveloped stretch of island covered in dense, low-growing woodland. The easternmost reaches are treasured by windsurfers, who seek out this point for its stronger winds.

Traveling on either road, you can reach the north side and turn back west to **Rum Point**, a fun-loving spot filled with watersports activities and dining. (A ferry from Seven Mile Beach brings visitors to this remote beach.) This is definitely the most "happening" spot east of George Town, a miniature version of Seven Mile Beach (without the hotels).

South of Rum Point lies **Cayman Kai**, one of the most lavish residential areas in Grand Cayman. This peninsula is lined with expensive homes and villas.

> **TRIVIA:** *"Going country" or "going to the tropical side" means a trip to the East End residential section.*

Getting Around

If you're staying on the East End or will be exploring this part of the island, you'll definitely want to rent a car. Taxi service is available on call to this region, but consider renting a car for more extensive travel.

Two-wheel enthusiasts will find this to be the best area in Grand Cayman for bicycle trips. The grade is flat and traffic is light.

Adventures

On Foot

The **Mastic Trail**, Frank Sound Road, ☎ (800) 949-1996. Grand Cayman's newest hiking trail is also one of its oldest. The 200-year-old Mastic Trail, a footpath once used by locals to herd cattle to the south coast, has been renovated and is open for guided tours through a two-million-year-old woodland area. The trail is a project of the National Trust for the Cayman Islands and winds through the Mastic Reserve.

The 200-year-old Mastic Trail.

The two-mile trail travels through swamps, woodland, and farming areas, with changing fauna along the way. One of the most interesting places is a region filled with fine red soil called "red mold." The dirt contains minerals found in the ancient rocks of Africa and scientists believe that dust from the Sahara Desert blew across the Caribbean and accumulated here. (It's not uncommon for hazy days to be attributed to sand blowing off the distant desert.)

Many visitors experience the trail with the expert guidance of Albert Hines, a young resident of North Side. Hines identifies birds along the way, often sighting the Grand Cayman parrot, Caribbean dove, West Indian woodpecker, Cuban bullfinch, smooth-billed ani, and the colorful bananaquit.

The 2½-hour hike also travels past 100 different types of trees, including black mangroves that grow from the brackish water, elegant royal palms, and tall mahogany trees. Fruit trees, first planted by early residents, include mango, tamarind, and calabash. Orchids bring color to the trees during the spring season, probably the best time of year to experience this eco-tourism attraction. Look for the wild banana orchids (the Grand Cayman version has cream-to-white blossoms with purple lips and the variety seen on the Sister Islands are pale to bright yellow with purple centers.)

The walk takes in several environments – from mangrove swamp to dry woodlands to an ancient forest – as it travels south to north. The forest contains over 100 species of trees and 550 other plant varieties. The trail was named for the mastic tree, once used by islanders for its lumber. Today, a tall Mastic tree can still be seen at the halfway point of the trail.

The eight-person guided tours are scheduled Monday and Friday at 8:30 a.m. and 3 p.m., and on Saturday at 8:30 a.m. only. Reservations are required and the cost is US $30 per person. The tour is not recommended for children under age six, for the elderly or those with physical disabilities. Wear sturdy shoes and bring insect repellent. Cold soft drinks and transportation back to the trailhead are provided. Call ☎ (800) 949-1996 or fax (345) 949-1996 between 10 a.m. and 3 p.m., Monday through Friday, for reservations. You can also E-mail the Trust at ntrust@candw.ky; check out the Web page at: www.cayman.com.ky/pub/ntrust/.

The National Trust doesn't advertise the trail's location. To reach the Mastic Trail, take Frank Sound Road north. Just past the fire station, take the first road left. Stay left and follow that dirt road 7/10th of a mile across several cattle guards. (If you head north on Frank Sound Road and reach the Botanic Gardens, you've gone too far.) A small parking area beside the Mastic Trail sign marks the trailhead. It can be hiked without a guide, although plants are not marked and the trail is not a loop, so plan to turn around and retrace your steps.

EARTH WATCH: *The purchase of the ancient forest seen along the Mastic Trail is just one project of the National Trust. Today the development plan includes protection of the Central Mangrove Wetland, 8,500 acres that flood during the wet seasons and are an important part of the natural Grand Cayman landscape. Over 7,000 acres of this wetland are privately held. To preserve this region, the National Trust is working to acquire parcels of the wetland and to conserve the region which is home to the whistling duck, parrots, snowy egret, and hickatees. The National Trust is encouraging donations for this project and can be reached at National Trust for the Cayman Islands, P.O. Box 31116 SMB, Grand Cayman;* ☎ *(345) 949-0121 or fax (345) 949-7494.*

Queen Elizabeth II Botanic Garden, Frank Sound Road, ☎ (345) 947-9462. One of the best (both economically and educationally) attractions on Grand Cayman is the Queen Elizabeth II Botanic Garden. The garden has two main features: the Woodland Trail and the Heritage Garden. Both offer distinct experiences. The trail emphasizes Cayman flora and fauna in a natural setting, while the garden showcases tropical plants from around the globe in a beautiful garden.

The Woodland Trail, just under a mile long, is a must-see for anyone interested in Cayman plants. Budget at least half an hour for the walk. More time will allow you to read the informative exhibits and look for turtles in the swampy undergrowth. Stop and listen for the call of a Cayman parrot in the trees.

The trail winds through several types of environments. One of the wettest is a swamp filled with the buttonwood, one of the few trees that can live with its roots continually submerged in water. The swamp provides humidity for bromeliads and orchids. On the other end of the spectrum, cactus country illustrates the dry regions of the Cayman Islands, and it's home to large century plants (agave) and cacti. One habitat is similar to that found on Little Cayman and includes flora found on the tiny Sister Island.

Grand Cayman

Birders should bring along binoculars for this walk. Commonly seen species include the Grand Cayman parrot, the northern flicker, vitelline warbler (a small yellowish bird found only in the Cayman Islands and on Swan Island), the zenaida dove, and the bananaquit.

Butterflies are another common sight. The caterpillars of the Cayman swallowtail (*Papilio andraemontaibri*) feed on lime trees; the white peacock (*Anarte jatrophae jamaicensis*) is the most commonly spotted along the trail.

Watch the shadowy undergrowth and you may spot some of Grand Cayman's most reticent residents as well. The agouti (*Dasyprocta punctata*), a shy rodent, is occasionally seen. Other residents include the hickatee (*Trachemys decussata*), a freshwater turtle found in the brackish ponds of the Cayman Islands and Cuba. The Grand Cayman blue iguana (*Cyclura Nubila Lewisi*) or the Cayman anole lizard (*Anolis conspersus*), with a blue throat pouch, are also seen. Grass snakes (*Alsophis cantherigerus*) feed on frogs and lizards, but are harmless to humans.

After a walk along the Woodland Trail, take time to visit the beautiful showplace gardens (see *Sightseeing*, below). The gardens are open 7:30 a.m. to 5:30 p.m. daily. Admission is US $3.12 for adults, US $1.20 for kids 6-12, and children under 6 are free.

Underwater

 Stingray City. The top watersports attraction in the Cayman Islands, Stingray City, is located in the mouth of the North Sound, halfway between the West Bay and the East End. Here, fishermen once cleaned their catch, attracting large Atlantic southern stingrays who are accustomed to being handled by participants in daily snorkeling excursions.

In 1987, *Skin Diver* magazine deemed this site "Stingray City" and since that time there's been no looking back. Stingray City is shared by many watersports operators, who offer half- and full-day excursions that include stops at both deep and shallow spots. Operators depart from all along the island for this adventure. The site is now one of the most popular in the Caribbean; often called "the world's best 12-foot dive," it can be enjoyed by both snorkelers and scuba divers.

Truly, this is one experience not to be missed. We have done the Stingray City experience several times using different operators and never leave disappointed. The trip out on the North Sound to the site is quick and scenic, but nothing can quite prepare you for the experience of petting, feeding, and being caressed by the stingrays. After mooring, some vacationers are a little cautious about heading into the waters (the stingrays are far less shy). We've noticed that all but the most nervous swimmer enjoys this experience.

On the shallow stop, the Sandbar, visitors stand (as still as possible to prevent kicking up sand and lowering visibility) while the stingrays swoop by, often brushing participants like some large rubbery frisbee. Operators begin the feeding and, as visitors become more comfortable with the process, others can feed and even hold the large rays.

Tour operators "play" with the rays.

Trips cost about US $45 per person and typically include three stops, the deepest of which is Stingray City at about 12 feet, followed by the shallower Sandbar, about three feet deep. Don't miss the chance to feed the rays some squid. Just pinch the squid between your fingers, arch your fingers back like you're about to slap someone, and put your hand down in the water: the greedy stingrays will do the rest. (If you don't arch your fingers back, the rays might suck up your fingers and give you a little scare. They don't have teeth, but their lips are a firm cartilage that will give you a jolt.) Typically about 30 stingrays frequent the area, so you're just about guaranteed the opportunity to pet and swim alongside these beautiful creatures.

After feeding the stingrays, most operators then take snorkelers over to Coral Gardens, a beautiful snorkel area with several large coral heads, fans, and abundant marine life.

STINGRAY CITY SCUBA OPERATORS

These excursions leave from all over the island (most along Seven Mile Beach) and many include free shuttle service from hotels and condos.

Abanks Watersports and Tours	☎ (345) 945-1441
Aqua Delights	☎ (345) 945-4786
Bayside Watersports	☎ (345) 949-1750
Black Princess Charters	☎ (345) 949-0400
(Seven Mile Beach)	☎ (345) 949-3821
Beach Club Hotel and Dive Resort	☎ (800) 482-3483
(West Bay)	
Bob Soto's Diving Ltd.	☎ (800) 262-7686
(locations on Seven Mile Beach	
Cayman Delight Cruises	☎ (345) 949-8111
Crosby Ebanks C&G Watersports	☎ (345) 945-4049
Don Foster's Dive Cayman Ltd.	☎ (800) 83-DIVER
Fantasea Tours, Seven Mile Beach	☎ (345) 949-2182
Frank's Watersports	☎ (345) 945-5491
(Seven Mile Beach)	
Kelly's Watersports, West Bay	☎ (345) 949-1193
Kirk Sea Tours and Watersports	☎ (345) 945-1611
(Seven Mile Beach)	
Ocean Safari Ltd., George Town	☎ (345) 949-6986
Oh Boy Charters, West Bay	☎ (345) 949-6341
Red Sail Sports, Seven Mile Beach	☎ (800) 255-6425
Scuba Sensations, Seven Mile Beach	☎ (800) 767-0445
Tourist Info. & Activity Services	☎ (345) 949-6598
(Seven Mile Beach)	
Wet 'n' Wild, Seven Mile Beach	☎ (345) 949-9180

Scuba Diving

While Stingray City may be deemed the world's best 12-foot dive, the East End offers plenty of other dive sites for all ability levels:

Julie's Wall: Set east of where Frank Sound Road intersects with the main road, this dive site is located 60 to 100 feet below the surface. An intermediate-level dive, the wall is home to black coral formations and rays are often spotted here.

The Maze: Located on the South Channel (not far from the Wreck of the Ten Sails), this is a honeycomb of tunnels that form a veritable maze. Best suited to intermediate and advanced divers, the site is 60 to 100 feet, but some of the passages lead far beyond that.

Snapper Hole: A 30- to 60-foot dive, this is a favorite with beginners, but still offers tunnels, plenty of marine life, and even an anchor from an 1872 shipwreck. The site is on the East End outside the reef that forms Colliers Bay.

Your author getting up close and personal with a friendly stingray.

Tarpon Alley: This wall dive of 60 to 100 feet is near Stingray City, just outside the North Sound. A favorite with underwater photographers, the alley has drop-offs, canyons, and, of course, huge schools of shiny tarpon.

Eagle Ray Pass: East of Tarpon Alley and across from the main channel into the North Sound, Eagle Ray Pass is named for the rays that are often sighted here. This wall dive runs 40 to 100 feet.

Grand Canyon: Situated near the Sandbar west of Rum Point, this 80- to 110-foot wall dive is for intermediate and advanced divers.

On the Water

 Rum Point. The tip of the East End is Rum Point, a peninsula that's home to willowy casuarina trees, chalky sand, aquamarine waters, and a club with just about every imaginable watersport. Recently, over $5 million was spent to improve this getaway spot, which now sports a full-service dinner restaurant, casual lunch eatery and bar, decks and walkways, plenty of comfy hammocks and picnic tables, a gift shop, and more.

The dock at Rum Point invites you to take a dip.

You can arrive at Rum Point by car (about an hour's drive from George Town) or on the *Rum Pointer Ferry*, which departs from the Hyatt Regency Grand Cayman. This 120-passenger ferry travels to Rum Point in about 30 minutes. For ferry reservations, ☎ (345) 947-9412. Ferry tickets are CI $6 each way; children 5-12, CI $3 each way; children under 5 travel free. (The price drops to CI $4 each way for 5:30, 7:30 and 9:30 p.m. departures.) If you're at Rum Point at dusk, don't miss the fish feeding off the docks.

FERRY SCHEDULE

Monday, Tuesday & Thursday:

Departs Hyatt	Departs Rum Point
9:30 a.m.	11:00 a.m
12 noon	1:00 p.m.
2:00 p.m.	3:00 p.m.
5:30 p.m.	6:30 p.m.
7:30 p.m.	8:30 p.m.
9:30 p.m.	10:30 p.m.

Wednesday, Friday, Saturday & Sunday:

Departs Hyatt	Departs Rum Point
9:30 a.m.	11:00 a.m.
12 noon	3:00 p.m.
5:30 p.m.	6:30 p.m.
7:30 p.m.	8:30 p.m.
9:30 p.m.	10:30 p.m.

Windsurfing

The **East End** is a top windsurfing area because of its stronger winds. Tradewinds of 15 to 25 knots blow during the winter months, dropping to 10 to 15 knots in the summer. Windsurfers find plenty of action inside the reef, while others choose to go out through the channel (be cautious of sharp coral when going through the channel). **Colier's Channel** is a good point to take the waves.

At Morritt's Tortuga Club (as well as close to Seven Mile Beach, near The Links of Safe Haven), **Cayman Windsurf** caters to both beginner and advanced windsurfers. Learn the sport, improve your knowledge, or just rent a craft and enjoy slicing through the water with the breeze. Beginners have four miles of reef-protected calm waters in which to learn and advanced practitioners can sail out through Collier's Channel. Prices average about US $30 for one-hour rentals or $75 per day; lessons run about US $40. For more details, call Cayman Windsurfing, ☎ (345) 947-7492 or fax (345) 947-6763.

On Wheels

The East End is excellent for cycling. A flat grade and little traffic make this a leisurely ride.

Eco-Travel

Birding

The best **birding** on Grand Cayman is found in this region, from the Mastic Trail to the Woodland Trail, at the Botanic Garden to **Meagre Bay Pond**, east of Bodden Town. Set off the main road, the large pond was once a popular hunting site and was abandoned by the teal and mallard that once populated the region in the early 1900s. However, the pond is now designated an Animal Sanctuary by the government and hunting is prohibited. Today, the bird population is beginning to climb once again.

Look for bats at the **Bat Cave**, outside Savannah at Spots Bay. The cave is a little tough to find, but if you're driving west on the way to George Town, take the first left on a dirt road past Pedro's Castle. Follow the dirt road to the sea, turn left and follow the cliff to a sandy beach. Climb down 10 feet to the small entrance of the cave (you'll have to crawl inside). If you can't find the cave, just stop and ask in Savannah.

Cultural Excursions

Pedro Castle. One of the East End's newest attractions is also its oldest. Pedro St. James Restoration Site, an 18th-century great house, has recently undergone complete renovation and today the building known as the "Birthplace of Democracy in the Cayman Islands" can be visited. Called Pedro Castle, the historic structure is situated in the community of Savannah, east of George Town.

The oldest known stone structure in the Cayman Islands, Pedro Castle was first built for William Eden, an early settler. In 1831, the house was the site of an historic meeting when residents decided that the five districts should have representation in the government. Four years later, a proclamation declaring the emancipation of all slaves was read at Pedro Castle and several other sites in the islands.

The restoration of the great house to its original 1820s condition has been a major undertaking, a US $6.25 million project. The site is at the center of a 7.65-acre landscaped park atop the 30-foot Great Pedro Bluff. For the past several years, historic research into the site has been conducted.

Bodden Town. History buffs can take a self-guided tour of Bodden Town, the city that served as the original capital of the Cayman Islands. Bodden Town is home of several historic sites, including the Queen Victoria Monument, a meeting site for men in the 1920s and 1930s to discuss politics, and Gun Square, just off the main road, where two 18th-century cannons once guarded the channel; today those cannons both point downward.

North Sound Beach Lunch. To learn more about Caymanian life, the North Sound Beach Lunch/Snorkeling Trip is offered by several operators. This trip also features snorkeling at either Stingray City or the Sandbar (depending on visibility and water conditions) and the Coral Gardens. The crew dives for pink queen conch, a shellfish that's then prepared as an appetizer, sliced and marinated in lime juice, onion and seasonings. Everyone goes on shore at Cayman Kai for a Caymanian lunch of peas and rice, potato or breadfruit salad, and local fish or spicy chicken. Part of the fun is talking with the captain and crew about Caymanian life. These trips cost $50 per person and run from 9 a.m. to 3 or 4 p.m.

NORTH SOUND BEACH LUNCH/SNORKEL TRIPS

Abanks Island Adventures, Ltd.	☎ (345) 949-5700
	fax (345) 949-0900
Bayside Watersports	☎ (345) 949-1750
	fax (345) 949-3700
Black Princess Charter	☎ (345) 949-0400/3821
	fax (345) 949-0391
Charterboat Headquarters	☎ (345) 947-4340

Grand Cayman

	fax (809) 947-5531
Best Value Charters	☎ (345) 949-1603
	fax (345) 949-0391
Capt. Crosby's/C&G Watersports	☎ (345) 947-4049
	fax (345) 947-5994
Captain Gleason Ebanks	☎ (345) 916-5020
	or 945-2666
Captain Marvin's Watersports	☎ (345) 947-4500
	fax (345) 947-5673
Cayman Delight Cruises	☎ (345) 949-6738/8385
Dallas Ebanks Watersports	☎ (345) 949-1538/916-2707
Ernie Ebanks Watersports	☎ (345) 949-1538/916-2707
Fantasea Tours	☎ (345) 949-2182
Frank's Watersports	☎ (345) 947-5491
	fax (345) 945-1992
Jackie's Watersports	☎ (345) 947-5791
	fax (345) 945-3762
Oh Boy Charters	☎ (345) 949-6341
Stingray City Charters	☎ (345) 949-9200
	fax (345) 949-3700

Sightseeing

Queen Elizabeth II Botanic Park, Frank Sound Road, ☎ (345) 947-9462. Situated about 25 minutes from George Town, the Queen Elizabeth Botanic Park is a 65-acre area filled with native trees, plants, and wild orchids, as well as birds, reptiles, and butterflies. (For more about the park's Woodland Trail, see *Adventures, On Foot*, above.)

The Visitors Centre, Heritage Garden and Garden of Flowering Plants are the newest additions to the gardens. The two-story Visitors Centre, built in traditional Caymanian architectural style, includes displays on natural history and botanical art, and small flower shows. A waterfall off the back of the center leads to a snack bar that serves sandwiches, patties, ice cream and juices.

Visit the Heritage Garden for a look at Cayman history. A Caymanian house from the East End has been restored and filled with donated furniture. The three-room structure was originally a family home where nine children were raised; today the yard is filled with the plants and fruit trees that a Caymanian family would have raised earlier this century. A cistern collects valuable rainwater and a separate kitchen keeps the heat of the stove and fire danger separate from the house. Beside the home, cassava, sugarcane, plantains, bananas, and sweet potatoes are grown in small open pockets in the lowland forest. Fruit trees are grown in soil found among the ironshore, much as they would have generations ago. Medicinal plants commonly grown around a Caymanian house, such as aloe vera, are found here.

The Garden of Flowering Plants is the most traditional botanical garden area here, with 2½ acres of floral gardens arranged by color. Pink, purple, orange, silver, and a whole rainbow of tones blossom with color and fragrance year-round. Overlooking the gardens and a small pond that features six-foot Victoria water lilies, a tea house has been constructed.

The gardens are open 7:30 a.m. to 5:30 p.m. daily. Admission is US $3.12 for adults, US $1.20 for kids 6-12, and children under 6 are free.

Pirates Cave, Bodden Town, ☎ (345) 947-3122. A less scenic and more touristy stop (but nonetheless fun) is at the Pirate Cave in Bodden Town. Reputed to have been used by pirates to hide their treasure and supposedly linked by tunnels to similar caves in the reef, the cave is now open for self-guided tours. You'll first view a blue iguana and Cayman parrot, as well as a traditional Cayman cottage, then head underground for a look at the cave. Across the street, alleged pirate graves, carved by slaves from rock in the shape of small houses, make an interesting site. Open daily 9 a.m. to 5 p.m. Admission is CI $3 for adults, CI $2.50 for children.

Stingray Brewery, Red Bay Road, ☎ (345) 947-6699. This micro-brewery produces the Stingray Beer, sold throughout the islands, and offers a tour of the brewery. Closed Sunday.

Blowholes. On the main road between Frank Sound and the East End, east of the turn off for Frank Sound Road, lies this roadside attraction. Park and walk down to the rugged coral rocks that have been carved by the rough waves into caverns. As waves hit the rocks, water spews into the air, creating one of the best photo opportunities on the island. You'll access the blowholes from a free parking area just off the main road; follow the wooden stairs down to sea level. Don't stand too close to the edge of these formations! The water shoots strongest when the waves are large (and the calmest days have no action at all), with sprays reaching 20 to 30 feet in the air. Wear good shoes for this excursion; the ironshore is sharp and footing isn't solid.

Prepare to get soaked at the blowholes.

Where to Stay

Hotels & Resorts

Cayman Diving Lodge, ☎ (800) TLC-DIVE, (345) 947-7555, fax (345) 947-7560. $$-$$$. Located 35 minutes east of George Town, this diving lodge is dedicated to dive enthusiasts, those whose vacation will focus on what lies beneath the waters. The lodge includes 17 guest rooms with air-conditioning, as well as a restaurant, bar, and gift shop. Two dive boats run to offshore wall dives and caves. Rates for a three-night package start at $368 in summer months.

Cayman Kai Resort, ☎ (800) 223-5427, (345) 947-9055, fax (345) 947-9102. $$. Cayman Kai is one of the island's most elegant, secluded areas. Just a short drive from Rum Point, it's also fairly close to the action if you prefer things to be a little busy. The 20 guest rooms at this small resort include air-conditioning, ceiling fans, TV, kitchenettes, and screened patios. The resort has a beach bar, dive shop, and tennis.

Morritt's Tortuga Club, ☎ (800) 447-0309, (345) 947-7449, fax 947-7669. $$. A favorite with divers and windsurfers, this East End resort is set right on the beach. Amenities include air-conditioning, ceiling fans, phones, TV, kitchenettes, pool, Jacuzzi, restaurant, bar, dive shop, scuba trips, snorkeling, sailing, windsurfing, fishing, and more.

Condos

Driftwood Village, ☎ (345) 947-9015, fax (345) 947-9138. $. Just four units mean that the pace is quiet and private at these condominium cottages. Rates start at $125 in the winter and fall to $95 during the summer months.

Where to Eat

American **Wreck Bar and Grille,** Rum Point, ☎ (345) 947-9412. $-$$. Dine on burgers, club sandwiches, patties, conch fritters, BBQ chicken salad, fisherman's salad, and jerk pork sandwiches in the comfort of your bathing suit. Table service to the beachside picnic tables makes this an enjoyable way to lunch on a relaxing Rum Point day.

Caribbean Pooh's Restaurant, East End, ☎ (345) 947-7427. $-$$. Located far down on the East End, this restaurant serves up English, American, and continental breakfasts. Lunch and dinner menus feature local cuisine.

Reef Point Restaurant and Lounge, Bodden Town (east of Pirate Cave), ☎ (345) 947-2183. $-$$. This eatery serves local dishes as well as pizza and snacks. It's well known for daily shark feedings at 6 p.m.

Grand Cayman

Seafood

The Lighthouse, ☎ (345) 947-2047. $$. Don't worry about missing this restaurant: just look for the first lighthouse on your right as you head out from George Town. Housed in a former lighthouse, this fun eatery serves lunch and dinner either indoors or outside. Along with a menu featuring seafood – conch chowder, jerk shrimp pitas, and seafood Caesar salads– several Italian dishes are offered as well.

Rum Point Restaurant, Rum Point, ☎ (345) 947-9412. $$-$$$. Open for dinner only, this eatery features island favorites like shrimp, lobster, and conch, as well as pasta dishes, prime rib, and chicken.

Seven Mile Beach

Introduction

This beautiful swath of white sand separates 5½ miles of hotels, condominiums, and restaurants from an aquamarine sea. Dotted with casuarina trees, this beach is the most popular spot on the island. Come here to watch and be watched, to enjoy an island concoction or to slather on oil and bake yourself into tropical bliss. Watersport operators line the way, offering anything from scuba trips and parasailing to windsurfing and jetskiing.

Seven Mile Beach runs south to north along Grand Cayman's western edge, stretching from George Town to a region called West Bay. Along Seven Mile Beach, Grand Cayman narrows to a skinny stretch about a mile wide, bordered by the beach on the west and the North Sound to the east. On its eastern boundaries, the sea makes an uneven boundary, at some points etching into the land with salt creeks and harbors. Much of these eastern reaches are covered by swampy vegetation.

The largest harbor along this stretch of the North Sound is **Governors Harbour**, where Governors Creek creeps into the land in a maze of natural and man-made canals. Today it's lined with luxury lots and lavish homes, as well as the Cayman Islands Yacht Club.

The beach faces West Bay and beyond it lies the Main Drop-Off, an area of the ocean that plummets to great depths. Protected marine parks run parallel to the shore, safeguarding delicate coral reefs and marine life. Measuring just 5½ miles, the name "Seven Mile Beach" may be somewhat of a misnomer. But in some ways the strip of sand seems much longer because of the numerous businesses packed along its expanse. The beach is public and you'll find beach access points scattered all along, sometimes sandwiched be-

Seven Mile Beach.

tween condominium developments. One of the best access points is the public beach park, tucked north of the Westin Casuarina Hotel. With plenty of parking (other beach access areas offer parking on the shoulder of busy West Bay Road), this is one of the best options for enjoying Seven Mile Beach if you're not staying at one of the area properties.

The park includes shaded pavilions, restrooms with changing rooms, and a small playground for the kids. Squeaky clean and, like the rest of the island, devoid of any beach vendors, the park is a wonderful place to spend an afternoon.

Getting Around

Take your pick on Seven Mile Beach: taxi or rental car, pedal or foot power. They're all good options.

Car Rental

A car is not necessary to enjoy Seven Mile Beach, but it is handy if you'd like to tour the entire stretch of beach and venture to other areas of Grand Cayman. Rentals are available at several nearby agencies; most offer free pickup and dropoff at Seven Mile Beach. Rentals begin at about US $30 per day. A temporary driver's license is required; you can obtain this from the rental agency by presenting a valid driver's license and paying the US $7.50 fee. You must be 21 or over to rent a vehicle; some agencies require renters to be 25 years of age.

For a full listing of car rental agencies on the Cayman Islands, see page 40.

Scooters

A popular way to buzz around the island is on a scooter. You must have riding experience to rent one; expect to pay about $25 per day. A permit is required.

Scooters are available for rent at several locations on Seven Mile Beach: **Cayman Cycle Rentals** (☎ 345-945-4021) has rentals at Treasure Island Resort, the Hyatt Regency Grand Cayman, and Coconut Place. **Soto Scooters and Car Rentals** at Coconut Place (☎ 345-945-4652) also offers scooter rentals.

Bicycles

Prices vary but average about US $12 per day for a 10-speed bike and $14 for a mountain bike. Note that traffic can be extremely heavy along West Bay Road during morning and evening rush hours.

Call **Cayman Cycle Rentals** or stop by the offices at Coconut Place on West Bay Road, the Hyatt Regency Grand Cayman, or Treasure Island Resort, all on Seven Mile Beach. Mountain bicycles are also available for rent from Cayman Cycle Rentals.

Soto's Scooters and Car Fun Rentals also rents bikes; ☎ (345) 945-4652.

Adventures

On Foot

Golf

 The Links at Safe Haven (☎ 345-947-4155, 947-4001 fax) is the only championship 18-hole golf course in the Cayman Islands. Rates average US $60 for 18 holes. Shoe and cart rental are available. Men are required to wear shirts with collar and sleeves; women must wear a shirt to cover shoulders. Golf carts are mandatory and operators must be at least 17 years old and have a valid driver's license. Cart rental runs US $20 per person. Services at the course include a golf pro for lessons, golf shop, putting greens, chipping and bunker practice areas, aqua driving range, open-air patio bar, and The Links Restaurant for lunch and dinner (reservations suggested; ☎ 345-949-5988). To book tee times, ☎ (345) 949-5988.

THE CAYMAN BALL

The goal of most golfers may be to drive the ball as far as it can go, but that task becomes a little more difficult with the Cayman Ball. Designed to go only half as far as a regular ball, this tricky orb make the best use of the small course area on the island. Britannia is the first course designed for use of the Cayman Ball.

At the **Hyatt Regency Grand Cayman**, the **Britannia Course** was designed by Jack Nicklaus. This links-style course, with the challenges of its seaside location, includes blind tee shots, pot bunkers, and two-tiered greens. On the fifth hole, golfers shoot over the Caribbean waters. This course can be played as a nine-hole championship course, an 18-hole executive course, or an 18-hole Cayman Ball course. For advance starting times, ☎ (345) 949-8020.

Underwater

Scuba Diving

 Just beyond the sand, much of Seven Mile Beach drops off into spectacular dive sites.

The Aquarium: With a name like The Aquarium, this 30- to 50-foot dive has to be good. Look for a wide variety of fish off the upper end of Seven Mile Beach. Goatfish, snapper, parrotfish, and more await on this beginner-level dive.

Wreck of the *Oro Verde*: About half a mile off the beach at Villas of the Galleon, the *Oro Verde* is a favorite with beginners because of its shallow position (25 to 50 feet). The ship was used by drug smugglers (*Oro Verde* means "green gold" in Spanish, so we'll let you draw your own conclusions about its cargo) and in 1980 was scuttled. Today, the gold lies in its rich marine life; the high that divers get from this myriad of color is a completely legal one.

On the Water

Watersports

 Non-divers can enjoy the undersea world aboard a glass-bottom boat. The *M.V. Reef Roamer*, a 34-foot, 26-passenger vessel, travels along Seven Mile Beach. It offers a look at both natural and man-made attractions below the water's surface, from colorful tropical fish and coral to shipwrecks usually viewed by scuba divers. The 1½-hour tour costs US $25; for reservations, ☎ (345) 947-4786. For more active fun on the water's surface, rent a waverunner from one of the operators along the beach. Prices average about US $40 for a half-hour. You'll find waverunners at Don Foster's **Dive Cayman** at the Marriott beach.

Sailing

Many watersports operators run sailing trips out to Stingray City (see *Adventures, East of George Town*). One of the largest operators is **Red Sail Sports Grand Cayman** (☎ 800-255-6425), located at the Hyatt Regency. Along with a full menu of water toys, from Hobies to waterskis to banana boats, Red Sail Sports also operates the *Spirit of Ppalu*. This 65-foot catamaran was originally built as a racer; it now cuts a sleek path through the waters of the North Sound, sailing to Stingray City, and also offering sunset cruises and dinner sails. The catamaran has a glass bottom for a sneak peak at what lies below. Red Sail Sports also operates four dive boats. We journeyed aboard the *Spirit of Ppalu* and enjoyed a quiet sail through the channels that lead out into the sound. In spite of choppy conditions that day, we had a smooth sail and would recommend the catamarans for anyone who is prone to seasickness; the twin hulls make for a smoother ride. Rates on the *Spirit of Ppalu* are US $60.50 for a sail to Stingray City, including lunch.

Windsurfing

Windsurfing is enjoyed along Seven Mile Beach, although real aficionados venture to more challenging waters elsewhere on the island. If you do windsurf at Seven Mile Beach, be on the constant lookout for swimmers and snorkelers (while snorkeling, we once had a near miss as one windsurfer skimmed by way too close). Prices average about $20 per hour for windsurfing and equipment can be obtained from Don Foster's **Dive Cayman** at the Marriott.

Windsurfing Operators

Sailboards Caribbean, ☎ (345) 949-1068
Located next to Plantana Condominiums, this operator is a Mistral certified school.

Cayman Windsurf, ☎ (345) 947-7492
Situated on the North Sound near the Links at SafeHaven (with another location on the East End at Morritt's Tortuga Club), this BiC Center welcomes beginners.

Sea Kayaking

Sea kayaks are a fun and fairly easy way to enjoy the water. Rent a kayak for an hour or two and paddle your way along the coastline, enjoying the casuarina-dotted strip of sand and a view of the accommodations that cling to this precious real estate. Sea kayaks for one and two people are available for rent from vendors for US $15-20 per hour.

In the Air

 The only **parasailing** in the Cayman Islands is offered along Seven Mile Beach. Soaring up high above the waves can be a thrilling adventure. Prices for parasailing average about $45.

PARASAILING OPERATORS

Abank's Watersports & Tours Ltd.   ☎ (345) 945-1444
Aqua Delights   ☎ (345) 945-4786
Beach Club Watersports   ☎ (800) 482-3483
Bob Soto's Diving Ltd.   ☎ (800) 262-7686
Cayman Skyriders   ☎ (345) 949-8745
   (Hyatt Regency and Westin Casuarina)
Kirk Sea Tours and Watersports   ☎ (345) 949-6986
   (Treasure Island Resort)
Red Sail Sports   ☎ (345) 949-8745
   (Hyatt Regency, Westin Casuarina)
Tourist Info. & Activity Services   ☎ (345) 949-6598

Cultural Excursions

 Visitors at the Hyatt Regency Grand Cayman Resort and Villas can get a glimpse into Caymanian history and customs in a new cultural program. Local experts introduce guests to traditional Caymanian activities – such as coconut husking, rope making, and weaving silver thatch palms into baskets and hats – while local historians recall the island's past.

"We are working closely with island historians and community artists to bring the real flavor and charm of the Cayman Islands to our activities," says general manager Doug Sears. "Culture is an important part of the island experience and, with these activities, guests will have a better understanding of island life." The resort also offers horticultural tours.

CRUISE SHIPS

Cruise ship call on George Town, Grand Cayman. Lines include: Carnival, Celebrity, Chandris, Costa, Crown Commodore, Crystal, Cunard, Epirotiki, Hapag Lloyd, Holland America, Kloster, Majestic, Norwegian Caribbean, Premier, Princess, Radisoon, Regency, Renaissance, Royal, Rotal Caribbean, Seaborn, Starlite, Sun Line and Ulysses.

Where to Stay

Seven Mile Beach boasts the lion's share of accommodations in the Cayman Islands. You'll find both luxury resorts and budget accommodations, lavish condominiums and economical motels. Not all accommodations are on the beach itself, but, with public beaches throughout, none are more than a few minutes' walk to the water.

Hotels & Resorts

Caribbean Club, ☎ (345) 945-4099, fax (345) 945-4443. $$. Eighteen one- and two-bedroom pastel pink villas offer seaside relaxation. Six of the villas are beachfront; others have a garden view. All rooms include a full kitchen, air-conditioning, ceiling fan, TV, phone, dining room, and furnished patio.

Grand Pavilion, ☎ (345) 945-5656, fax (345) 945-5353. $$$. One of Grand Cayman's most lavish hotels, resembling a Southern plantation, the Grand might be a little stuffy for some vacationers. The hotel includes two restaurants, two bars, a gym, 24-hour room service, and other services aimed at business and convention travelers. Not the place you want to drag into with the impression of a snorkel mask stamped into your face, dripping seawater and sand.

Hyatt Regency Grand Cayman, ☎ (800) 233-1234, (345) 949-1234; fax (345) 949-8528. $$. One of Grand Cayman's most beautiful resorts, the Hyatt is located on both sides of the road. It has a private beach club with full watersports. You may recognize parts of this resort from the movie *The Firm* (it's where Gene Hackman and Tom Cruise stayed).

"THE FIRM"

The first look that many visitors had of Grand Cayman was in the 1993 movie *The Firm*, starring Gene Hackman, Tom Cruise, Holly Hunter, and Jeanne Tripplehorn. The film included 350 local Caymanians as extras and prominently featured sites around the island.

Many of the scenes were shot at the Hyatt Regency. The pool bar, the garden, Loggia Lounge, the front drive, and other spots around the property were included in the film. Except for Tom Cruise, who rented a private home, the stars stayed at the Hyatt Regency and Britannia Villas.

The crew members were stationed down at the Sleep Inn and George Town Villas, and the Paramount offices were set up in what's now the Clarion Grand Pavilion. Other locations that appear in the movie include:

◆ Cheeseburger Reef: Check out the characters of Avery and Mitch scuba diving this shallow west coast site during their first stay on the island. (Hackman and Cruise actually did the dive shot themselves. Bob Soto's Diving Ltd. provided the watersports services for the film and their Holiday Diver custom dive boat was repainted as "Abanks Dive Lodge.")

◆ George Town: The intersection of Harbour Drive and Cardinal Avenue was the location of a phone booth that the Gene Hackman character uses as Mitch (Cruise) first sees the Abanks Dive Lodge advertisement.

◆ Abanks Dive Lodge: This set was constructed on North Sound in Newlands. The site is still standing.

◆ Holiday Inn Pool Bar: Listen for the background music of the Barefoot Man in this scene.

◆ Hyatt Regency Aquas Pool Bar: The Jeanne Tripplehorn character surprises Avery (Hackman) at this bar.

Movie buffs, enjoy!

The 235-room hotel includes many levels of rooms and suites plus luxury villas. With landscaping as beautiful as a botanical garden, the hotel flows from a great main house to grounds dotted with royal palms and ponds filled with colorful koi, and a freeform swimming pool, complete with bridges and pool bar.

All rooms have air-conditioning, mini-bar, satellite TV, coffee-makers, telephones, and more. Resort facilities include four restaurants and five bars, private beach club, pool and hot tub, dive shop, 24-hour room service, watersports, dive shop, golf, health club, beauty spa, and more. Several packages are available.

Divers can enjoy a three-night stay in an island-view room with two-tank morning dives daily, one night dive, a sunset cruise, Rum Point ferry excursion, and one round of golf for $819 in highest season (January through mid-April), $575 in low season (June through September). Non-divers can deduct $209 from the package price. Other packages include scuba school for new and advanced divers, golf, and honeymoon.

Grand Cayman

EARTH WATCH: *The Hyatt Regency Grand Cayman offers a unique cultural program to introduce guests to the island's history, culture, flora and fauna. Horticultural tours, led by the resort's landscaping experts, point out sea grape, travelers' palm, silver thatch palm, and more. For a peek at the island's past, visitors can talk with a local historian. For more hands-on experiences, a coconut husker teaches the secrets of obtaining the edible portions of this thick fruit, while local artists show the skills needed to make rope, baskets and hats from silver thatch palms.*

The Great House, ☎ (800) 235-5888, (345) 945-4144, fax (345) 949-7471. $$$$. This third-floor apartment, used by *The Firm* filmmakers, includes three bedrooms and a den that can become a private fourth bedroom. It has one king, one queen, and two twin beds, plus two day beds.

Kitchen with microwave, 3½ baths, satellite TV and VCR, dishwasher, icemaker, wine cellar, washer/dryer, dining room, and beachfront balcony are found in the apartment as well. Guests have use of a freshwater pool, tennis courts, and gym on premises. This luxury accommodation is rented with a minimum of a one-month stay and the price is princely: US$30,975 per month.

Indies Suites, ☎ (800) 654-3130, (345) 947-5025; fax (345) 947-5024. $$. Although it doesn't have a beachfront location, Indies Suites is a good choice if you're looking for suite accommodations. All rooms include either a king-size or two double beds and a full-size kitchen equipped for four. They also have satellite TV, telephone, storage locker for dive gear, and a convertible sofa bed.

The family-operated all-suites hotel has a dive shop and an introductory scuba diving course is free. There's a pool, hot tub, cabana bar, boutique, mini-mart, and complimentary continental breakfast daily.

Marriott Grand Cayman, ☎ (800) 223-6388, (345) 949-0088; fax (345) 949-0288. $$. Located two miles from George Town and about four miles from the airport, this convenient property (formerly the Radisson) sits on a beautiful stretch of Seven Mile Beach. Swimmers and snorkelers can enjoy calm waters and a small coral reef just offshore or learn scuba diving or book dive trips through the on-site shop. Oceanfront rooms include private balconies with good beach views and are worth a somewhat long walk to the elevators in this 315-room hotel. Facilities include casual and fine dining, pool and hot tub, dive shop, waverunners, windsurfing boards, shopping arcade, and a full-service spa.

Sleep Inn, ☎ (800) SLEEP INN, (345) 949-9111; fax (345) 949-6699. $$. If you're just looking for a centrally located place to lay your head after a day of fun in the sun, the Sleep Inn is a good choice. This chain motel is just outside of George Town along the Seven Mile Beach stretch (the hotel itself is not on the beach). Rooms have air-conditioning and telephones. The property has a pool and whirlpool, poolside bar and grill, dive shop, and watersports center.

Treasure Island Resort, ☎ (800) 327-8777, (345) 949-7777, fax (345) 949-8489. $$. This 280-room resort includes an offshore snorkel trail. Now starting to look a little tired around the edges, the hotel nonetheless has a pretty pool area with waterfall cascading down from the third-floor restaurant. Facilities include two freshwater pools, two whirlpools, tennis, dive operation, shopping, informal dining, bar and lounge.

Westin Casuarina Resort, ☎ (800) 228-3000, (345) 945-3800; fax (345) 949-5825. $$$. The newest hotel in Grand Cayman is built on a strip of beach bordered by willowy casuarina trees. The hotel has 340 guest rooms, most

Westin Casaurina.

with breathtaking views of the sea from step-out balconies. It has the feel of a conference property, with a slightly dress-up atmosphere in the main lobby. Facilities include beachfront, casual and fine dining restaurants, pools, whirlpools, tennis, fitness facilities, beauty salons, masseuse and masseur. Rates are, as would be expected in a resort of this caliber, pricey.

TRIVIA: *The casuarina trees found along the Westin's beach have long been used by fishermen offshore to get their bearings.*

Condos

Avalon Condominiums, ☎ (345) 945-4171, fax (345) 945-4189. $$$$. These oceanfront properties each offer three bedrooms and three baths. Designed with tropical decor and each with a large, screened lanai overlooking Seven Mile Beach, the condos each include cable TV, fully equipped kitchens, and laundry facilities; guests have use of a fitness center, lighted tennis courts, freshwater pool, and Jacuzzi. Daily maid service is available except on Sundays and certain holidays. From mid-December through mid-April, a seven-night minimum is enforced.

Discovery Point Club, ☎ (345) 945-4724, fax (345) 945-5051. $$. This beachside condominium complex offers 45 suites. The one- and two-bedroom apartments have air-conditioning, screened porches or balconies, telephone, and TV. Units have kitchens, but some garden-view hotel-type units are available without kitchens. Facilities include Jacuzzi, pool, and tennis. Children under six stay free.

Grand Bay Club, ☎ (800) 825-8703, fax (345) 945-5681. $$. This 21-unit complex is quiet and peaceful, with well-furnished rooms that have air-conditioning, telephones, TV, VCRs, kitchens, laundry facilities, and maid service. Tennis, fishing, and snorkeling available.

Plantana Condominiums, ☎ (345) 945-4430, fax (345) 945-5076. $$. This 49-unit complex offers elegant condominium accommodations just steps from the beach. Two- and four-guest units are available, all with air-conditioning, ceiling fans, telephones, television, kitchens, maid service and laundry facilities.

Seven Mile Beach Resort and Club, ☎ (345) 949-0332, fax (345) 949-0331. $$$. Located inland but with private beach facilities, this condominium property has two-bedroom, two-bath units. Each has private balcony, air-conditioning, telephone, cable TV, VCR, and a fully equipped kitchen. The complex includes a freshwater pool, Jacuzzi, lighted tennis court, outdoor grills, and childrens' play area. Seven Mile Watersports arranges trips to Stingray City and has complete dive facilities, including resort and certification courses. Rates for one to four people (children under 12 free).

Villas of the Galleon, ☎ (345) 945-4433, fax (345) 945-4705. $$ (two to six guests). Within walking distance of Seven Mile Beach hot-spots, this 74-unit complex is popular for its well-furnished units. Rooms include air-conditioning, telephone, TV, VCR, kitchen, laundry facilities, and maid services.

Where to Eat

The Cayman Islands offer a wide variety of dining options, especially Grand Cayman, where visitors can opt for anything from a three-course gourmet meal to fast food. Typically, vacationers should expect to pay about US$45-75 per person for a three-course meal with wine in one of the island's finest restaurants; about US$6-10 for a casual lunch or dinner. Fast food lunches or snacks can be obtained for about US$3-7 per person.

American

American Eats Crocodile Rock Café, Falls Shopping Mall on West Bay Rd., ☎ (345) 947-5288. This American-style diner starts with a full breakfast then moves on to serve daily lunch specials, including burgers, soups, salads, sandwiches and fajitas. Dinner offerings run from stir-fry dishes and steak to seafood, and pasta.

Caribbean Café Tortuga, West Bay Rd., ☎ (345) 949-8669 or 949-7427. $$. Sit inside in the faux-Caribbean atmosphere or outdoors on a very faux-sand "beach" and enjoy reasonably priced breakfast, lunch, or dinner at this restaurant owned by Tortuga Rum. Menu selections include many Caribbean favorites – jerk chicken with rice and peas is popular – along with steaks, burgers, pizza, pastas, fish burgers, and much more. It's all followed, not too surprisingly, by dessert selections that include a slice of that not-to-be-missed Tortuga Rum Cake. Service here can be glacial, but reasonable prices make it worth a visit.

Lantana's Restaurant and Bar, West Bay Rd., ☎ (345) 947-5595. $$$. This elegant restaurant has an excellent menu featuring spicy Cuban black bean soup, jerk pork tenderloin, grilled yellowfin tuna with cilantro linguine, and more. Top it off with tropical coconut cream pie with white chocolate and mango sauce or frozen Cayman lime pie with raspberry sauce and whipped cream. Inventive presentations make this a good choice for a special night out.

Lone Star Bar, West Bay Rd., ☎ (345) 945-5175. $-$$. This bar, next to the Hyatt Regency entrance, was recently named one of the "World's Top 100 Bars" by *Newsweek* magazine. The atmosphere is rollicking and fun, a mix of both locals and vacationers who come to enjoy a drink and some conversation in this t-shirt decorated bar. Every inch of available space seems to be occupied by the donated t-shirts as well as autographed memorabilia. The Lone Star is often patronized by visiting celebrities. The adjoining restaurant, decorated as a 50s diner, features an All-You-Can-Eat Fajita Rita night on Monday and Thursday, a Cayman bargain.

Continental

The Links Restaurant, The Links at Safehaven Golf Course, ☎ (345) 949-5988. $$$. Located upstairs in the golf club, this air-conditioned restaurant is a favorite with duffers for both lunch and dinner. The lunch menu offers fried scampi, fish and chips, burgers, and steaks. Dinner includes a wide variety of dishes, from salmon steak to Jamaican jumbo shrimp to veal schnitzel and Brazilian pork. Open for lunch from 11:30 to 2:30; dinner 6 to 9:30.

Fast Food

It may not seem right to come to the islands and dine on fast food, but budget-conscious travelers find this is a valuable option. We found the fast food chains, while offering American food, did offer a slice of local life – most fellow diners are local residents. We also found the service to be friendly and prompt; Pizza Hut provided excellent table service and a kind staff member transformed a penny-pinching night out into a nice dinner for the two of us. Fast food franchises found along Seven Mile Beach include Burger King, KFC, Pizza Hut, Taco Bell, and others.

Italian

Ristorante Bella Capri, West Bay Rd., ☎ (345) 945-4755. $$. Enjoy seafood or Italian specialties at this casual eatery. Veal and steak round out the menu. Open for lunch 11:45 to 2 p.m. on weekedays; dinner 5:30 to 10:30. Reservations are suggested.

Seafood

Seafood Benjamin's Roof Seafood Restaurant, West Bay Road at Coconut Place, ☎ (345) 947-4080. $$$. When you're ready to go all out, head to this elegant restaurant which serves clams casino, marinated conch, turtle steak, lobster, shrimp, crab, scallops, and a full line of meat and pasta dishes. Open for dinner from 5:30 to 10:30; an early bird menu is offered from 3 to 5:30 p.m.

Shopping

Although not as extensive as the shopping in George Town, even the most dedicated shopper will find plenty of diversion along West Bay Road.

Coconut Place, across from the Villas of the Galleon, and **Galleria Plaza**, just south of the Hyatt Regency, are some of the top shopping areas. Look for duty-free liquor, jewelry, island clothing, and other vacation purchases along this strip. (For really serious duty-free shopping, head to George Town.)

Grand Cayman

Nightlife

As many visitors rise early for morning dives, nightlife in the Cayman Islands is generally quiet. The most activity is found along Seven Mile Beach, however, where you can club-hop, enjoy some live bands, and even take in a comedy show.

Treasure Island Resort is also popular for nightly entertainment, with Long John Silver's Nightclub and Tradewinds Lobby Bar, featuring a steel drum band.

The young crowd enjoys action at **Sharkey's Boca Bar** (☎ 345-945-5366). The **Planet Nightclub** (☎ 345-949-7169) rocks with soca, calypso, salsa, and reggae and has sports night every Monday.

Sunset cruises are another popular way to wind down the day. *The Cockatoo* (☎ 345-949-7884 or 949-7621) offers sunset sails for CI $20. The two-hour cruise starts at 5 p.m. and free pick-up and drop-off at area hotels is available. BYOB welcomed. *The Spirit of Ppalu* (☎ 345-949-8745) departs from near the Hyatt Regency for cocktail and dinner cruises.

If you're ready to enjoy a quiet, cool evening, catch a film at **Cinema I & II** on West Bay Road (across from the Marriott); ☎ (345) 949-4011 for listings and times.

NAUTILUS SUBMARINE

Although Grand Cayman has long been the home of the *Atlantis* submarine, it is now home base for the Nautilus (☎ 345-945-1355). Since April, this 80-foot semi-submersible submarine, docked at Calico Jack's in George Town, has provided a one-hour tour to view the rich marine life of the bay. The sub goes out about three-fourths of a mile offshore offering visitors a chance to view two shipwrecks and to watch a diver feed a variety of tropical fish. Good for families with children and for anyone claustrophobic. Tours are offered at 10:30 a.m. and 2:30 p.m. daily, with additional tours scheduled on Tuesday, Wednesday, and Thursday mornings as needed. The tours are priced at $35 per person and $19 for childrens.

The Nautilus also offers a unique tour on Thursday evenings. The Murder Mystery Theater is scheduled from 6:30 to 8 p.m. and includes a professional actor who interacts with the audience in trying to solve a "murder" on board. Unlimited hors d'oeuvres as well as beer, wine, and rum punch are available throughout the evening. These tours are priced at $43.75.

West Bay

Introduction

Vacationers along fun-loving Seven Mile Beach miss the "real" Grand Cayman, a place where homes, not condos, line quiet streets. Where children grow up in cozy neighborhoods. Where friends take time from their day to stop and say hello or to sit out in the yard and just enjoy a Caribbean afternoon.

That feeling of real life is found in West Bay, directly north of Seven Mile Beach, but a much greater distance away in terms of atmosphere. Don't look for slick swimwear shops or shipwreck jewelry here. Hotels are few. But West Bay, like the East End, is for visitors looking for the real Grand Cayman.

The shape of West Bay somewhat resembles a hammer head perched atop the hammer handle of Seven Mile Beach. The head of the hammer is the most developed area of West Bay. Here you'll find the **Cayman Turtle Farm** and numerous dive sites. Traveling north from Seven Mile Beach along West Bay Road, the name of the road changes to North West Point Road and follows the coastline, leading past an area that becomes more and more residential. At the Cayman Turtle Farm, a less traveled road traces the far northern edge of this region, continually switching names along the route: Boatswains Bay Road, King Road, Birch Tree Hill Road, Conch Point Road, Palmetto Point Road. Traveling west, houses become fewer and fewer and the area gives way to a swampy habitat that's a favorite with birds.

Or you can turn away from the coast and head to the inland area of West Bay to a community called **Hell**, a popular stop on island tours. Located, appropriately enough, on Hell Road, this small town cashes in on its unusual moniker with the expected t-shirt shops and a post office that sends off postcards franked with the obligatory Hell postmark. Nevertheless, it's a small, homey community that's worth a visit.

Hell doesn't look so threatening on Grand Cayman!

Follow Hell Road East onto Reverend Blackman Road and then Batabano Road to travel to the North Sound and the fishing community of Batabano. This is home of **Morgans Harbour**, starting point for many deep-sea fishing cruises and some tours of Stingray City. It's not as glitzy as Seven Mile Beach, but offers an interesting look at a working side of Grand Cayman.

Back to the hammerhead image: The claw of the hammer is the Barkers area of West Bay. Located north of Batabano, **Barkers** is also popular with birders, who find good sites off Palmetto Point Road on its northern reaches and along its many ponds.

Getting Around

If you plan to move around while on this end of the island, you'll want a **car. Taxi service** is available, but rates from West Bay down to other parts of the island are not cheap. A taxi from Spanish Bay Reef Resort on the far north side of West Bay to the airport area of George Town runs $27, one way.

Walking and **bicycling** are other good options in this region. With quiet, neighborhood streets throughout much of this section, you'll find good opportunities for foot and pedal power.

Adventures

On Foot

A **walking tour** of central **West Bay** is available from the National Trust. The 37-stop tour begins at the West Bay United Church and continues on to many historic sites. Some of the most interesting architectural styles are pointed out on buildings along the way, including the wattle and daub houses typical of those built on the island from the 17th through the early 19th centuries. Handmade using few tools, the homes were built of mahogany, ironwood, wattles, daub, and thatch and had outdoor bathrooms and kitchens as a safety feature. Wattles are woven wood panels covered by a coral lime plaster substance called daub. Making the daub was often a neighborhood-wide activity since it was so labor-intensive. Coral rocks were broken up and baked in a large kiln to create lime ash. This was mixed with sand and water then daubed onto the wattles, usually about six inches thick. Although a fairly simple construction method that used all locally available materials, this style was sturdy and could withstand the hurricanes and tropical storms as well as rain and sun.

Wattle and daub houses built from the mid-19th century to present are called manor houses. Showing American influences, the modern homes have indoor baths and kitchens as well as verandas.

Timber houses, constructed of imported lumber using ship-building tools, were constructed starting in the mid-19th century. The most striking feature of these homes was their intricate fretwork or gingerbread trim. Later, the bungalow style was a favorite, using pre-cut lumber and later cement and blocks.

Traditional Caymanian sand gardens are unique. Raked clean, the sand gardens are often trimmed with conch shells and have paths paved with coral.

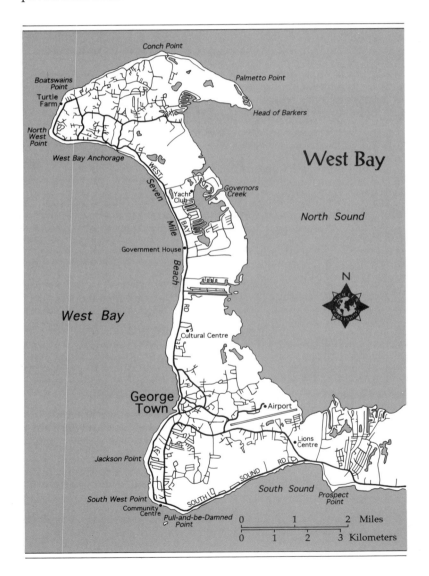

Underwater

Scuba Diving

 The West Bay area has some of the best scuba diving sites in Grand Cayman:

Bonnie's Arch: Just off North West Point, this 50- to 70-foot dive is a favorite with underwater photographers because of its arch formation, which is covered with corals and sponges. Good for beginners, the dive offers even more than the spectacular arch, with many types of marine life, from tarpon to tangs.

Hepp's Pipeline: This 30- to 60-foot dive for beginners and intermediate divers is not far from the Cayman Turtle Farm. It has two mini-walls and can be a shore dive.

Big Tunnel: Swim-throughs and canyons and a depth of 60 to 100 feet make this a favorite with intermediate and advanced divers. Located off the North West Point (close to Bonnie's Arch and the Orange Canyon).

Orange Canyon: A 60- to 100-foot dive, the canyon is favored by intermediate and advanced divers. This wall dive is filled with color and is named for its orange elephant ear sponges. Near Bonnie's Arch.

Trinity Caves: Located in West Bay, the caves sit at 40 to 100 feet. Beginners can enjoy a look at spectacular corals and fans, while intermediate and advanced divers can enter the three channels that wind their way to a wall where large species might be spotted. Look for turtles on this dive.

Ghost Mountain: At North Point, West Bay, you will see a large coral pinnacle, the base of which lies on a sand slope at a depth of 140 feet. Large schools of jacks swim in and out of the cave at the base. This 70- to 100-foot wall dive is for intermediate to advanced divers.

Spanish Bay Reef: Walk right out to this shallow reef dive (30 to 60 feet) near Spanish Bay Reef Resort. This site is also good for snorkeling (although the waters can be rough).

Turtle Farm Reef: Just east of the turtle farm, a short swim from the shore, this site offers a steep mini-wall rising from a 60-foot sand bottom. You can do this as a shore dive or enjoy this site as a snorkeler.

Snorkeling

One of the top snorkel spots on the island is located near the cemetery. Follow West Bay Road north from Seven Mile Beach. As the road begins turning west into West Bay, you'll see a small cemetery between the road and the sea. Nearby, there's public access to the beach and it's a short swim from here to **Cemetery Reef**.

Another popular snorkel spot is the **Turtle Farm Reef**. It's just a short swim from the shoreline and offers snorkelers a look at a mini-wall and abundant marine life.

These West Bay operators offer guided snorkel trips of either a full or half-day. They provide a good opportunity to travel to the reefs beyond the reach of shore swimming. Great for beginners to get an introduction.

WEST BAY SNORKELING OPERATORS

Capt. Marvin's Aquatics	☎ (345) 945-4590
Cayman Delight Cruises	☎ (345) 949-8111
Jackie's Watersports	☎ (345) 945-5791
Kelly's Watersports	☎ (345) 949-1193
Oh Boy Charters	☎ (345) 949-6341
Resort Sports Limited	☎ (800) 482-DIVE
Seasports	☎ (345) 949-3965

On Horseback

Most horseback riding on the island is along the powdery beaches, an excellent place for practiced riders to romp and gallop and for beginners to enjoy a slow walk on cushioned sand (a comfort to those who feel they may fall off). Both experienced horsemen and those new to the sport can enjoy beach rides, trail rides, and, with a 24-hour notice, a ride including a beach picnic with **Pampered Ponies** (☎ 345-945-2262). Two locations, on Batabano Road and Barkers, offer rides starting at US $40. If you're on the island at the right time, don't miss a full moon ride.

Sightseeing

Cayman Turtle Farm, West Bay, ☎ (345) 949-3893/3894. The chief sightseeing stop on the West Bay is also one of the island's most popular. The world's only turtle farm, it had over 260,000 visitors last year. Since 1968 this unique farm has offered visitors the chance to get up close and personal with green sea turtles.

Named for the color of their fat, some of the green sea turtles weigh 700 pounds and can be viewed slowly swimming in open-air tanks in the center of the farm. You'll even have the opportunity to pick up one of the small reptiles. Allow about 45 minutes at the farm, which makes an excellent rainy day distraction. The turtle farm has been both praised and criticized for its operation. Many turtles are released into the sea every year from this farm, although others find their way onto Cayman dinner tables.

A baby turtle up close.

Turtle meat served at local restaurants comes from the Cayman Turtle Farm. The farm defends its efforts and points out that by providing turtle meat – a longtime Caymanian favorite – to the local market, it diminishes the need for turtle hunting. Also, the survival rate at the farm is much higher than in the wild. Here, nine out of every 10 turtles survive, as compared to one out of 10 in the wild.

The turtle farm displays the life cycle of the green sea turtle from birth through breeding stage. A nursery shows where the eggs, which are laid by the big breeder turtles on a sand beach at the farm, are incubated. The hatchings live in tanks and are fed high-protein pellets similar in appearance to dog food. This diet accounts for the rapid growth of the farm's turtles compared to their relatives in the wild.

The self-guided tour of the turtle farm takes you past many tanks filled with turtles in various life stages. A special tank contains turtles that you may pick up and hold, an excellent photo opportunity. Reach down and clutch the turtle's body just behind his front flippers. He'll flip and flap around, trying to swim away in mid-air, unless you hold him vertically.

The prime resident of the Cayman Turtle Farm is the green sea turtle, the most common turtle in the Cayman Islands. The farm is also home to several other turtle displays, including the following.

◆ Hawksbill turtle (*Eretmochelys imbricata*). With a narrow, sharply serrated carapace and a bird-like bill, the hawksbill turtle is easy to identify. Specimens range from 90 to 180 pounds.

◆ Kemp's Ridley sea turtle (*Lepidochelys Kempi*). The most endangered of the sea turtles, these are being raised at the farm for future release into the wild.

◆ Loggerhead turtle (*Caretta caretta*). Found off the Florida, Georgia, and Carolina coasts, these weighty (200 to 350 pound) turtles have large heads that give them their name.

The farm also recognizes the land residents of the Cayman Islands in several exhibit areas. Look for the agouti (*Dasyprocta*) or the Cayman "rabbit" in one area. These rodents, found in the eastern districts of Grand Cayman, have long, thin legs, hoof-like claws, and three toes on their hind feet (five toes on the forefeet). Once a food source, today the rodents are rarely spotted. Nearby, another display area houses the American crocodile. Early verbal records speak of sightings of this 20-foot crocodile (*Cocodylus acutus*) in

Grand Cayman and Little Cayman; recent archaeological finds have proven this claim.

Admission to the farm is US $6 US for adults, US $3 for children six to 12 (under six free). The farm is open daily 8:30 a.m. to 5 p.m.

TURTLE TRIVIA

The sex of green sea turtles is dependent on the temperature during incubation. At 82°, an equal number of males and females are born. If the temperatures are cooler, all males are produced. At warmer temperatures, the hatchlings will all be female.

Only one mature turtle is expected to survive from an average 10,000 eggs in the wild.

Mating season for green sea turtles lasts from April through July; the pair may mate for as long as six days.

Nesting season occurs from May through October.

At the turtle farm, single individual turtles have laid as many as 690 eggs in a single clutch. A female may nest one to 10 times a season, producing up to 1,700 eggs in a year. She may nest every year or skip several years.

Mature green sea turtles have been observed to stay several days underwater without surfacing for air.

Hell. East of the turtle farm lies an attraction that is pure Hell. This odd attraction is actually a community named Hell, a moniker derived from the time an English commissioner went hunting in the area, shot at a bird, missed, and said "Oh, hell." The name must have seemed appropriate for the devilishly pointed rocks near town, a bed of limestone and dolomite that through millions of years have eroded into a crusty, pocked formation locally called ironshore.

To reach this small community, follow West Bay Road north from Seven Mile Beach. At the intersection of Town Hall Road, turn right and continue to Hell Road. Turn left to this small town.

Meet the devil in Hell.

Today, Hell trades upon its unusual name as a way to draw tourists to the far end of West Bay. Visitors stop at the post office (and the three shops directly adjacent) to buy postcards and have them postmarked from Hell. Nearby, The Devil's original post office ships out its share of postcards. The store is manned by Ivan Farrington, who dresses as the devil himself to greet tourists who come to buy the obligatory postcard and other Hell-related gifts, from hot sauces to t-shirts.

Step behind the store or the post office for a close-up look at the ironshore that gave this region its unusual name. Even with all the Hades-related attention this small community draws, a stroll along its streets will show that this is a heavenly quiet town. And, yes, you'll see that there are indeed churches in Hell.

Conch Shell House. Interesting as a drive-by attraction, the conch shell house is included on most island tours. It's privately owned so you can't enter the premises, but the North Sound Way attraction is often photographed. Handmade from conch shells, it's charming and certainly one of the most picturesque homes in the Caribbean. Ask locally for directions.

Where to Stay

Hotels & Resorts

Spanish Bay Reef, ☎ (345) 949-3765, fax (345) 949-1842. $$. Located on the far northwest end of West Bay, Spanish Bay Reef is a good choice for those seeking an all-inclusive package. Tucked on a sandy stretch of beach shaded by tall palms and willowy casuarina trees, the resort is casual and fun. The sea here is somewhat choppy, although a barrier creates a swimming area, but this resort is a favorite with divers. Dive sites include No Name Wall, Chinese Wall, Lemon Drop-Off, Grand Canyon, The Pinnacles, and more, each offering a peek at an undersea world filled with marine life, fascinating formations, and beautiful corals.

All rooms have air-conditioning and private balcony or patio and satellite TV. The resort features the Spanish Main Restaurant and Calico Jack's Poolside Bar as well as a private beach, freshwater pool, Jacuzzi, and dock.

The all-inclusive package covers all meals and beverages (well drinks only, no wine or champagne), use of sightseeing cars on a shared basis, bicycle, introductory scuba and snorkeling lessons, unlimited scuba diving from shore for certified divers (including tanks and weight belt), boat dives (usually a two-tank dive), airport transfers, and all taxes and gratuities. The three-night diver package (standard room) starts at $684 per person ($585 for non-divers) and includes two boat dives. Low season rates, from the end of June through August, drop to $616 for divers and $527 for non-divers.

Condos

Magnificent Dive Dump, ☎ and fax (345) 949-3787. $ (up to three guests). With a name like this, who couldn't like this little place? It has only five units but low prices keep dedicated divers coming back. Located on the northwest end of West Bay, these condos offer shore diving and snorkeling and a dive operator on site. Rooms have air-conditioning, ceiling fans, telephone, TV, kitchens, and maid service.

Grand Cayman

Guest Houses

White Haven Inn Guest House, ☎ (345) 949-1064, fax (345) 945-4890. $. Located on Batabano Road in a quiet residential neighborhood, this modest guest house offers a slice of real Caymanian life at a reasonable price. Three guest units feature air-conditioning, ceiling fans, telephone, televisions, and VCRs. A full American breakfast is included, along with free airport pick-up. After a day out scuba diving and exploring the island, guests can enjoy quiet walks in this neighborhood, where cattle peacefully reside in large fields.

Where to Eat

Italian

Ristorante Pappagallo, Conch Point Rd., ☎ (345) 949-1119 or 949-3479. $$-$$$. The beauty of this restaurant hints at the specialness of a meal here. A thatch roof, made from over 100,000 thatch palm leaves, shields a building designed from bamboo, local stones, and marble. Parrots, cockatoos, and macaws lend their voices to create an exotic atmosphere that's echoed in the setting: the restaurant is perched on the shores of a small natural lake in a bird sanctuary.

Meals here are special, featuring northern Italian cuisine. Homemade pastas, seafood, and fine wines make this restaurant well worth the drive for those staying in the Seven Mile Beach area. Dinner is served from 6 to 10:30 p.m. daily.

Caribbean

Liberty's, West Bay, ☎ (345) 949-3226. $-$$. For a real taste of local food, come by Liberty's, an eatery that bills itself as a "native style restaurant." All-you-can-eat buffets on Wednesday, Friday, and Sunday draw diners for conch stew, turtle stew, barbecue chicken, curry chicken, rice and beans, and more. Lunch is served daily 11:30 to 4 p.m.; dinner served 6-10.

Seafood Cracked Conch by the Sea, Northwest Point Rd., West Bay, ☎ (345) 945-5217. $$. Next door to the turtle farm, this restaurant must be relying on its position to draw business. Even by Caymanian standards, drinks are expensive (CI $6 or US $8 for a rum punch). The restaurant is popular for its all-you-can-eat specials, but we never found out how good it was: the manager insisted that all outdoor tables were reserved... even though three-fourths were vacant.

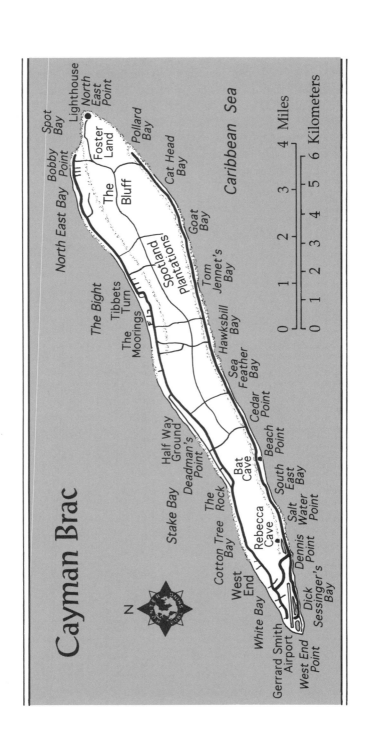

Cayman Brac

N

Caribbean Sea

Lighthouse
North East Point

Spot Bay

Bobby Point

Foster Land

Pollard Bay

North East Bay

Cat Head Bay

The Bluff

Goat Bay

Spotland plantations

Tom Jennet's Bay

The Bight

Tibbets Turn

The Moorings

Hawksbill Bay

Sea Feather Bay

Cedar Point

Beach Point

Half Way Ground

Deadman's Point

Bat Cave

South East Bay

Stake Bay

The Rock

Cotton Tree Bay

Rebecca Cave

Salt Water Point

Dennis Point

West End

White Bay

Dick Sessinger's Bay

Gerrard Smith Airport

West End Point

0   1   2   3   4 Miles

0   1   2   3   4   5   6 Kilometers

Cayman Brac

If Grand Cayman is the flashy big brother of the Cayman Islands, swelled with pride about its lavish condominiums, full-service resorts, international dining, and top-notch diving, and Little Cayman is the family's youngest sibling, favored for its petite size and almost shy demeanor, then Cayman Brac is the middle child. Have no fear, though; this middle sibling is not at all overlooked.

Cayman Brac has its own special qualities, assets that include world-class diving along undersea walls, hiking in the most rugged terrain found in the Cayman Islands, caves that tempt exploration, birding, sunning, and much more.

The island is named for the "brac," Gaelic for bluff, which soars up from the sea 140 feet on the island's east end. It's the most distinct feature of this 12-mile-long, one-mile-wide island that sits 89 miles east-northeast of Grand Cayman and just five miles from Little Cayman.

With a population of under 2,000 residents, Cayman Brac is closer in pace to Little Cayman. Residents, or Brackers, are known for their personable nature and welcome vacationers to their sunny isle.

Cayman Brac is a long, eel-shaped island that starts with the **Gerrard Smith Airport** on its westernmost end near a town named, appropriately enough, West End. This end of the island is also home to most guest accommodations and the island's only beaches.

Two roads etch the perimeters of the island. A6 traces the northern coast, starting at West End and working past Knob Hill, Banksville, Half Way Ground, Molusca Heights, Tibbetts Turn, and Spot Bay. Along the way, the road looks out on a sea that hides several good dive sites beneath its placid waters.

On the southern shore, A7 traces its way from West End Point all the way northeast, journeying past the island's resorts, Brac Reef

Beach Resort and Divi Tiara Beach Resort, past several good caves that are favorites with outdoor adventurers, and up to **Pollard Bay**.

A small center road works through the center of the island, and this is the route to Cayman Brac's best known attraction: the **bluffs** or the Brac.

Getting Around

AIRPORT CAR RENTAL COMPANIES

Avis/Cico	☎ (345) 948-2847
Brac-Hertz Rent-a-Car	☎ (345) 948-1515
Four D's Car Rental	☎ (345) 948-1599

Adventures

On Foot

Hiking

Some of the best hikes include walks up the 140-foot-high Bluff. Rocky paths snake their way up the Bluff; wear hiking boots for this challenge.

On the lower Bluff area, you'll also find some challenging hikes that cut through rugged bush. Just look for road signs that appear without roads. They point the way to brush trails once used by farmers that are today enjoyed by hikers looking for a challenge. Bring along water for these excursions. Most of the trails average about 1½ miles, but can take considerably longer than you might expect due to the dense foliage.

Another good option is the nature trail in Cayman Brac's Parrot Reserve. Located atop the Bluff, this newly opened trail is great for self-guided tours. The trail is a mile long and takes hikers through the Parrot Reserve, which is home to the endangered Cayman Brac parrot. For more information, contact Wallace Platts, chairman of the trust's district committee, at ☎ (345) 948-2390.

Caving

The Bluff is pocked with caves that frame beautiful seaside views. No one really knows the history of these caves. Some guess that pre-Columbian Indian settlements used them; others say they were the lair of plundering pirates who used their dark recesses to hide their loot. None of these legends has been proven, but one use of the caverns is known for certain. During the Great Hurricane of 1932, the caves offered shelter for many Brackers.

Several of the 18 caves on Cayman Brac have been explored. Five are frequently visited by vacationers:

Rebecca's Cave. Located east of Divi Tiara Hotel, this cave is marked with signs. The best known of the island's caves, sadly this one is named for a young child who died here during the Great Hurricane of 1932.

Skull Cave. On the north coast near the high school and east of Faith Hospital lies this interesting cavern.

Peter's Cave. This cave requires either a climb down a steep path or a hike downhill, so bring along good shoes for this task. From the cave, you can view the community of Spot Bay below.

Bat Cave. On the south side of the island, this two-level cave is marked with signs.

Great Cave. Also on the south side, Great Cave also requires a steep climb.

> **TRAVEL TIP:** *Visitors to Cayman Brac should bring along a pair of old jeans for exploring caves and a pair of old sneakers with good soles for walking on the ironshore beaches.*

Cayman Brac

Underwater

Scuba Diving

 Without a doubt, the diving off Cayman Brac is one of the island's prime attractions. Over 50 prime dive sites tempt all levels of divers.

The latest attraction is a Russian frigate deliberately sunk in September 1996. Renamed the *M/V Captain Keith Tibbets*, this 330-foot freighter was built for use by the Cuban navy. It lies approximately 200 yards offshore northwest of Cayman Brac. The bow rests in about 90 feet of water; the stern is just 40 feet below the surface. This is Cayman's first wreck dive site to allow multi-level computer wreck diving experience. The site is marked with three permanent dive moorings.

Before sinking the vessel, the ship was modified to be safe for divers. Divers can now swim through the upper three decks, although the hull and lower decks cannot be entered. Divers can see into most of the ship and should be able to spot the missile launcher, fore and aft deck cannons, and living quarters.

It doesn't take long for marine life to discover additions to their underwater home; already divers have spotted eagle rays, stingrays, Queen angelfish, filefish, four-eyed butterfly fish, puffer fish, batfish, snapper, red soldier fish, sergeant majors, French grunts, barracuda, jacks, and more.

The sinking of the vessel was recorded by Jean-Michel Cousteau Productions in a documentary film, *Destroyer of Peace*.

Anchor Wall: Located on the south side of the island off Dennis Point, this wall dive is considered intermediate level. Don't miss the anchor of an old Spanish galleon; it marks the entrance to a tunnel leading to a vertical wall that drops into the deep blue abyss.

Charlie's Reef: On the north side of the island near Cotton Tree Bay, this 20- to 60-foot dive is a favorite with beginners and is named for a green moray.

Inside Out: This wall dive off South East Bay is a favorite with beginners because of its shallow (15 to 50 feet) depth. With coral heads, a tunnel, and plenty of marine life, it's a good choice for anyone.

Radar Reef: Off Half Way Ground on the island's north side, this shallow dive can be reached from shore and is a favorite for night diving. Look for octopus!

East Chute: This all-level dive, located on the north side of the island in White Bay, has something for everyone. Wreck divers will find the remains of a 65-foot vessel in its waters; those looking for spectacular formations will find canyons and tunnels.

Scuba Operators

Brac Aquatics Ltd
☎ (800) 544-BRAC
For 20 years this operator has offered dives for all levels. Three dives are offered daily with a 14-diver maximum. PADI and NAUI affiliated.

Peter Hughes Dive Tiara
☎ (800) 367-3484
This PADI 5-star dive and photo center leads visits to over 50 sites on Cayman Brac and neighboring Little Cayman. Located at the Divi Tiara Beach Resort, it also offers photo and video rentals. PADI, NAUI, SSI, and NASDS affiliated.

Reef Divers
☎ (800) 327-3835
At Brac Reef Beach Resort, this dive service includes a full photo and video center. Three dives daily; 20-person maximum. PADI, NAUI, SSI, and NASDS affiliated.

Cayman Brac

Snorkeling

The wreck of the *M.V. Captain Tibbets* can be enjoyed by snorkelers. Located just a short swim off shore, the wreck sits in 50-100 feet of water and is already home to a good selection of marine life.

Snorkel operators include: **Capt. Frankie Bodden,** ☎ (345) 949-1428; **Shelby Charters,** ☎ (345) 948-0535; and **Southern Comfort,** ☎ (345) 948-1314

On the Water

Fishing

Try your luck fishing for tarpon or enjoy a few hours of bonefishing with one of these guides:

Brac Caribbean Beach Village
☎ (800) 791-7911
Groups of up to four people can book a full or half-day of deep-sea fishing or bone, tarpon, and reef fishing.

Capt. Edmund "Munny" Bodden
☎ (345) 948-1228
In operation 38 years, this guide specializes in bone fishing. Up to four fishermen can book a full- or half-day of either deep-sea or bone, tarpon, and reef fishing.

Capt. Frankie Bodden
☎ (345) 949-1428
Located at Divi Tiara Beach Resort, Captain Frankie has been in business 31 years and offers full- or half-day deep-sea fishing trips for up to six persons aboard a 30-foot Phoenix.

Shelby Charters
☎ (345) 948-0535
Captain Shelby Scott offers full- and half-day excursions – either deep-sea or reef fishing – for up to eight participants.

Southern Comfort
☎ (345) 948-1314
Captain Lemuel Bodden has offered fishing
excursions for 25 years. Full- and half-day deep-sea
trips available.

In the Air

Day Trip to Little Cayman

 Hop aboard with Island Air for a 15-minute jaunt over to
Little Cayman, a popular day trip from Cayman Brac.
With twice daily service, **Island Air** (☎ 345-949-5252,
Monday through Friday, 9 a.m. to 5 p.m.; fax 345-949-7044) offers
round-trip fares for just US $40. Special fares are available for
children under age 12. The day trip is a favorite with bone fisher-
men and scuba divers who will both find operators on Little
Cayman willing to accommodate day visitors.

INTER-ISLAND FLIGHT SCHEDULE

Cayman Brac to Little Cayman
    Departs 9:30 a.m.; arrives 9:45 a.m.
    Departs 5:20 p.m.; arrives 5:35 p.m.

Little Cayman to Cayman Brac
    Departs 8:55 a.m.; arrives 9:10 a.m.
    Departs 4:45 p.m.; arrives 5 p.m.

On Wheels

 A good driving tour has been compiled by the National
Trust. A 40-minute cassette audio tape takes visitors on
a self-guided drive around the island. You can obtain the
tapes from AVIS (☎ 345-948-2847) for a small rental fee or purchase
a copy for CI $10 from the Cayman Brac National Trust district
committee.

Eco-Travel

Birding

Birdwatching is a favorite activity on Cayman Brac. Several sites are popular for sighting some of the island's most sought-after species: **Saltwater Pond** on the southwest coast, best known as the home of the West Indian whistling duck; and the **Parrot Reserve**, located on the Bluff. This 180-acre preserve is home to many of the endangered Cayman Brac parrot. Only 400 of the birds remain in the wild on this island. The best time to spot the emerald green parrot is July through September. They're often spotted on top of the Bluff, as well as around Stake Bay.

During the winter months, birders can look for peregrine falcons. Other top birding times are the spring and winter migrations, in February and March, and November and December. Birders are challenged by about 120 species, including the brown booby, Vitelline warbler, and the white-tailed tropicbird.

The Parrot Reserve is also a good destination for those interested in the flora and fauna of the island. Thirty-eight plant species can be seen here; a two-mile trail is open for self-guided hikes. Look for candlewood, mastic, wild banana orchid plants, and other exotic species along the trail.

EARTH WATCH: *To learn more about Cayman Brac's ecology and to assist in preservation efforts, consider becoming a member of the National Trust's Cayman Brac District Committee. For information, contact Wallace Platts at ☎ (345) 948-2390.*

Sightseeing

The **Cayman Brac Museum**, ☎ (345) 948-2622. This charming museum recalls the early history of this seafaring island. Located in the former post office, the museum houses ship-building tools, photos, and even a replica of a turtle schooner. The museum is open

Monday through Friday from 9-12 and 1-4 p.m. and on Saturday from 9-12. Free.

The Brac, East Point. This sheer bluff is Cayman Brac's most notable feature and worth a visit by hikers and non-hikers alike. To reach the Bluff, follow the gravel road north off Ashton Reid Road, the island crossroad. The gravel road runs six miles to a lighthouse.

Cayman Brac Community Park, West End. This park includes a short nature trail that identifies about 10 types of indigenous trees. Dedicated by Governor Michael Gore in 1995. Open daily.

Where to Stay

Hotels & Resorts

Brac Caribbean Beach Village, ☎ (800) 791-7911, (345) 948-2265, fax (345) 948-2206. $-$$. Located at Stake Bay, this 16-room resort has air-conditioning, ceiling fans, telephones, televisions, as well as restaurant, bar, scuba, a dive shop, snorkeling, and tennis.

Brac Reef Beach Resort, ☎ (800) 327-3835, reservations office (813) 323-8727. $. This 40-room resort overlooks Channel Bay on the island's southeast shore. Guest rooms have air-conditioning, ceiling fans, telephones, televisions, and porches or patios. The resort also offers a pool, Jacuzzi, restaurant, bar, scuba, dive shop, snorkeling, fishing, tennis, underwater photo center and gift shop.

Divi Tiara Beach Resort, ☎ (800) 367-3484, (345) 948-1553, fax (345) 948-1316. $-$$. Cayman Brac's largest resort offers 59 guest rooms, both standard and deluxe. Guest rooms feature air-conditioning, ceiling fans, telephones, televisions, and porches or patios. The resort also has a pool, Jacuzzi, restaurant, bar, scuba, dive shop, snorkeling, fishing, tennis, underwater photo center and gift shop.

Condos & Apartments

La Esperanza, ☎ (345) 948-0531, fax (345) 948-0525. $-$$. Visitors can choose from a two-bedroom apartment or a three-bedroom house. Located on the island's north side near The Bight, this property has a restaurant/bar. La Esperanze is not beachfront. Guest accommodations do offer air-conditioning, ceiling fans, and telephones plus kitchens and laundry facilities.

Small Inns

Walton's Mango Manor, ☎ and fax (345) 948-0518. $. Cayman Brac's first bed and breakfast is within walking distance of the Cayman Brac Museum. The community of Stake Bay and both snorkeling and shore diving are accessible. Walton's Mango is housed in an historic Caymanian house that formerly operated as a retirement home for Bracker seamen. Today, it's a five-room guest house. Rooms include air-conditioning, ceiling fans, telephones, and television; each has a private bath. A full breakfast is served daily.

This B&B is a favorite with nature lovers. Named for a large mango tree in the front yard, the garden features guinep, breadfuit, buttonwood and poinciana trees as well. Cayman Brac's parrots are sometimes spotted here.

Guests have use of a barbecue, patio and microwave; rental bicycles are also available.

Where to Eat

Aunt Sha's Kitcken, West End, ☎ (345) 948-1581, $-$$. Order up a plate of fresh seafood cooked with island spices at this charming eatery.

Edd's Place, West End, ☎ (345) 948-1208, $. Chicken and fish are the specialties most any day you visit.

G&M Diner, West End, ☎ (345) 948-1272. $. Local fish tops the menu at this diner.

La Esperanza Restaurant and Bar, Stake Bay, ☎ (345) 948-0531. $-$$. Located on the island's north side near The Bight, this casual eatery specializes in local seafood.

Little Cayman

Vacationers looking for secluded scuba diving, fly or tackle fishing, and nature appreciation find that Little Cayman fits the bill. Appropriate to its name, Little Cayman is only 10 miles long and two miles at its widest point. Boasting none of the glitz of Grand Cayman, 80 miles to the southwest, Little Cayman does greet guests with all the basic comforts, including several small lodges and condominiums with air-conditioning, satellite television, and telephone service.

This island is truly for those looking to get away from it all. Don't come here expecting even a fraction of the action found on Grand Cayman. Shopping is nil, nightlife hasn't even been considered. But for those seeking solitude, this is the place to be.

Introduction

Little Cayman was once the home of a few die-hard anglers and scuba divers who were willing to live without any creature comforts. One of the earliest residents was actor Burgess Meredith, who had a vacation home on the northwest side of the island in the 1970s, back in the days when electricity was produced only by home generators. (The first electrical service came to the island in 1991.)

With a permanent population of just over 100 people, the island's primary residents are birds and iguanas.

Iguanas have the right of way.

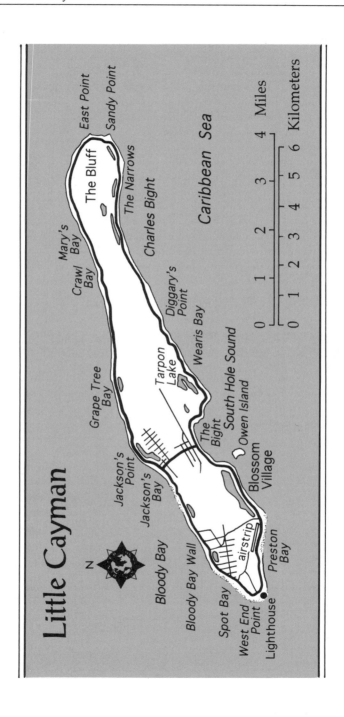

Little Cayman

Over 2,000 Little Cayman Rock Iguanas inhabit the island, so many that "Iguana Crossing" and "Iguana Right of Way" signs are posted throughout the island to protect the five-foot-long lizards. Local artists Janet Walker and John Mulak painted the popular signs.

Most of the island's residents live on its southernmost tip near a community called **Blossom Village**. Here you'll find island services, including the airport, car rental, grocery store, gas station, real estate office, restaurant, and several accommodations. The island's main road carves through town, but there's certainly no need to worry about traffic. So little happens on this island, in fact, that there's only one policeman (but locals warn that he's happy to use his new radar speed gun) and one taxi (but the driver has another job, so don't expect to be picked up at a moment's notice).

Past the main road, side streets wind through Blossom Village, curving past cheery neighborhoods where everyone knows one another and visitors are greeted with waves and smiles. A small cemetery, many of its graves marked with conch shells and white crosses bleached even whiter by the Caribbean sun, marks the final resting place of former Little Cayman residents.

Parallel to Blossom Village stretches a protected marine park, with some of the top snorkeling and dive spots on the island. Here divers find Grundy Gardens, Windsock, Harlod's Holes, Jay's Reef, Charlie's Chimney's, Patty's Point, Pirates Reef and Preston Reef, each the location of myriad marine life and underwater formations. Several dive operators offer trips to popular sites.

Beyond Blossom Village, the main road, known formally as Guy Banks Road on the southern stretch of the island, winds north past scrubby brushland. Soon the road passes the **Booby Pond Nature Reserve**, a brackish mangrove pond. Trees are dotted with white birds, the red-footed boobies, and overhead the distinct shape of the magnificent frigate bird can been seen soaring on the tradewinds.

Continuing north, **Owen Island** is soon seen off to the right. This uninhabited island spans just 11 acres but is a popular day trip destination for picnickers, who can reach the island's sandy beaches by row boat.

The bay to the north of Owen Island is known as **South Hole Sound** and this inlet marks one of the few intersections on the island. Here

Little Cayman

the Crossover Road, or more formally Spot Bay Road, crosses to the other side of the island.

Continuing north, the main road soon loses its pavement and gives way to packed dirt and sand, safe for all vehicles. Stay on the road, however, because deep sand is found at some turnoffs. Along this stretch you'll pass many shallow ponds on the left side of the road, each lined with low-growing vegetation that forms a home for the island's bountiful bird population. Birders enjoy a drive by **Tarpon Lake**, a brackish lake filled with tarpon and a favorite spot with anglers. The tarpon caught here range from three to 15 pounds. Birders will find more of interest along the pond's shoreline.

Tarpon Lake.

Scrubby undergrowth becomes thick as you work your way to the north side of the island, climbing a slight rise. This is the island's driest end, a place where the terrain becomes marked with tall cacti and century plants (agave).

Swimmers and picnickers find an excellent spot at **Point of Sand**, a.k.a. Sandy Point. Turn right off the main road where you see a stop sign at the approaching road. The sand is packed for the first half of the drive, but be sure to stop at the wide section, as it soon turns to deep sand. Do not attempt to take vehicles down. It's a long walk back to town and there are no facilities or telephones in this park.

This beach, luminescent with beautiful pink sand, is one of the island's prettiest and also most secluded. You very well might spend the entire day on this stretch of beach and never see another person. On weekends visitors from Cayman Brac often come over to enjoy the beach. A covered picnic table invites you to enjoy a quiet lunch with the sound of the sea as background music.

Beyond Sandy Point lies the **East Point**, the easternmost point of the island. From here you can

Picnic shelter at Sandy Point.

see nearby Cayman Brac seven miles across the channel. This stretch of Little Cayman is nearly deserted, with just a few cacti overlooking acres of undeveloped land.

The road then turns back south and traces the northern coast of Little Cayman, a stretch that's one of the favorites with divers. By far the most popular area is Bloody Bay Wall, found near where the Crossover Road comes out on the north coast road. This stretch of coastline is a marine park, safeguarding what has often been called one of the best dive locations on the globe. For many years, Little Cayman's most famous resident, actor Burgess Meredith, had a vacation home along this coastline.

> **TIP:** *To sound like a local when saying Little Cayman, pronounce Cayman with an emphasis on the last syllable.*

Little Cayman

Getting There

Arrival on Little Cayman is half the fun – you land in a cloud of dust. The dirt airstrip is next to a tiny one-room building that shades a desk and a phone; this is the Edward Bodden Airport. With twice-daily service from Grand Cayman, **Island Air** (☎ 345-949-5252, Monday through Friday 9 a.m. to 5 p.m.; fax 345-949-7044) departs on the 45-minute flight at 8 a.m. and 3:50 p.m.; return flights depart at 9:55 a.m. and 5:45 p.m. Round-trip tickets are US $122 (US $98 for passengers under 12); a day trip package is also available for US $105 (US $84 for travelers under 12). Passengers may check up to 55 lbs of baggage free of charge; excess baggage is charged US 50¢ per pound.

Flights are also available on Island Air from Cayman Brac to Little Cayman and cost US $40, round-trip. Special fares are available for children under age 12.

INTER-ISLAND FLIGHT SCHEDULE

Grand Cayman to Little Cayman
Departs 8 a.m.; arrives 8:45 a.m.
Departs 3:50 p.m.; arrives 4:35 p.m.

Little Cayman to Grand Cayman
Departs 9:55 a.m.; arrives 10:40 a.m.
Departs 5:45 p.m.; arrives 6:30 p.m.

Cayman Brac to Little Cayman
Departs 9:30 a.m.; arrives 9:45 a.m.
Departs 5:20 p.m.; arrives 5:35 p.m.

Little Cayman to Cayman Brac
Departs 8:55 a.m.; arrives 9:10 a.m.
Departs 4:45 p.m.; arrives 5 p.m.

Getting Around

Car Rentals

Only one rental car agency operates on the island. **McLaughlin Jeep Rental** (☎ 345-948-1000, fax 345-948-1001) offers daily and weekly rates for jeeps; only standard transmission jeeps are available. To call the rental agency on arrival, pick up the phone located on the side of the airport building. Vehicles are left-hand drive; driving is on the **left** side of the road. Rates start at US $59 daily. A Caymanian driver's permit is required for rentals; obtain one at McLaughlin's for a US $7.50 fee. There is a 25 mph speed limit throughout the island.

Bicycling

Another popular mode of transportation is the bicycle. Guests will find that most resorts provide complimentary use of bicycles and, with practically no traffic on the roads, they offer a peaceful way to see the island, journey to a secluded beach, or pop into Blossom Village. The old cycles may not be the fastest vehicles, but, after all, this is Little Cayman. What's the hurry?

Adventures

On Foot

Departing from Salt Rock Bay (across from the dock on the north side of the island), the mile-long **Salt Rock Nature Trail** winds through natural habitat and is a favorite hike for birders and those interested in Little Cayman fauna. Look for the 17 endemic species plus orchids, bromeliads, cacti, and mahogany trees. Iguanas, blue land crabs, curly tailed lizards, and many of the island's bird species are spotted as well.

Little Cayman

The trail winds past the old railroad that was constructed to serve a former phosphate mining business. Another highlight is Pirates Well, a cave fed by a freshwater well. Discovered in 1994, the cave has not yet been fully explored.

Guided tours of the island are led by Gladys Howard, National Trust Chapter Chairman and owner of the Pirates Point Resort. Tours are conducted every Sunday morning; for more information contact the **Cayman Islands National Trust, ☎** (345) 949-0121, or Gladys Howard, ☎ (345) 948-1010. A CI $1 donation to the Little Cayman National Trust is asked.

Aside from guided hikes, Little Cayman presents travelers with plenty of walking and hiking opportunities. Almost non-existent traffic, a flat grade on all but the island's easternmost end, and wide roads make Little Cayman perfect for a stroll or hike. Stroll the quiet streets of Blossom Village, the main road out to Tarpon Lake, or the island's beautiful beaches.

Underwater

Scuba Diving

 Little Cayman's unmatched dive opportunities provide the island's greatest draw. Along its 10-mile length, 57 dive sites are marked with moorings. The most famous site is Bloody Bay Wall on the north side of the island. The wall drops off just a short swim from the shore at a depth of only 20 feet, making it a favorite with snorkelers as well.

Scuba Operators

Paradise Divers
☎ (800) 450-2084
Groups of up to 16 can be accommodated by this facility, which offers three dives daily.
Complimentary beverages. PADI affiliated.

Pirates Point Resort
☎ (800) 327-8777
Located at the resort, this dive shop offers two
dives daily for groups up to 20 divers. PADI, NAUI,
and SSI affiliated.

Reef Divers
☎ (800) 327-3835
Little Cayman Beach Resort is home to this facility,
which includes a full-service photo and video
center. Three dives offered daily for groups of up to
20 divers. PADI, NAUI, SSI, and NASDS affiliated.

Sam McCoy's Fishing & Diving Lodge
☎ (800) 626-0496
Located at the lodge on Little Cayman's north shore,
this operator runs excursions to the Bloody Bay Wall
as well as shore diving along Jackson's Point. PADI
and NAUI affiliated.

Southern Cross Club
☎ (800) 899-2582
This fishing and diving resort leads four dives daily
for small groups (no more than 10 divers). PADI,
NAUI, and SSI affiliated.

Best Dive Sites

Bloody Bay Wall: Starting at a depth of just 25 feet, this site is
nonetheless a favorite with divers of all skill levels and is considered one of the best dive sites in the Caribbean. Named one of the
top dive sites by the late Philipe Cousteau, the wall is thick with
sponges and corals and also home to many formations – chimneys,
canyons, coral arches. The wall is a spectacular sight, dropping
sheer into blackness from the clear turquoise shallows just inches
away.

Nancy's Cup of Tea: Located on the north side of the island off Big
Channel, this dive site begins a depth of just 35 feet before plunging
into deep waters. Decorated with multicolored sponges as well as
gorgonians. Look for lots of marine life here.

Meadows: West of Nancy's Cup of Tea, this shallow site is home to eagle rays, groupers, and more. Small caverns and overhangs make this spot special.

Marilyn's Cut: Off Grape Tree Bay on the north side of the island, the cut or crevice leads to a wall filled with sponges and gorgonians. This site is also home to a favorite resident: Ben, a Nassau grouper.

Randy's Gazebo: Out from Jackson's Point, Randy's Gazebo is noted for its tunnels and swim-throughs. This wall dive includes a natural arch that's a favorite with underwater photographers.

Snorkeling

Bloody Bay Wall: See description above.

These operators offer snorkel trips: **Sam McCoy's Fish & Dive Lodge,** ☎ (800) 626-0496; **Southern Cross Club,** ☎ (800) 899-2582.

On the Water

Fishing

 Fly and light tackle fishing attract anglers to the waters of Little Cayman, which offer excellent bonefishing in the shallow flats. Other anglers come to catch tarpon in the brackish Tarpon Lake or permit, a fish that weighs as much as 35 lbs and is also caught in the flats. Little Cayman is the top destination of the three Cayman Islands with those looking for light tackle and fly-fishing.

Bonefishing is a favorite activity and a challenge to anglers (although the sport here is not on a par with other islands in the Caribbean or the Florida Keys). These fish are seen in the shallow areas called muds, places where the sea is churned up by the bottom feeding fish.

Guides recommend baiting with fry. Bonefish can be caught all day although, like other types of fishing, the success rate depends on factors such as weather and tides. The best bonefishing around Little Cayman is usually found at the South Hole Sound.

Tarpon fishing is also popular on Little Cayman. Tarpon Pond, a brackish lake north of Blossom Village, is home to many 20-lb tarpon. Fly-fishermen will have best luck at this site in early morning and late afternoon.

Permit are also a favorite catch, ranging from 15 to 35 pounds. They're found in schools on the southeast end of Little Cayman and on the northwest coast flats.

Whether you're staying on the island or coming over on a day trip, you can enjoy some fishing with a local guide if you make advance arrangements.

MOLLY THE MANTA

A favorite resident of Little Cayman was Molly the Manta, a giant manta ray often seen on night dives in this region. With a 12-foot span, the manta was spotted along the north coast and on the south coast flats from 1991 through 1995. She was seen off Bloody Bay swooping through the water, scooping up plankton that were attracted by divers' lights. Today Molly is no longer spotted on night dives, but is believed to have reached maturity and gone off in search of a mate.

Fishing Operators

Sam McCoy's Fishing and Diving Lodge
☎ (800) 626-0496
McCoy's Lodge has guides on staff year-round. Sam McCoy has been leading fishing excursions on this island for 30 years and son Chip McCoy is widely considered the best light tackle fishing guide on the island. He also offers fly-fishing. Fishermen should bring their own fly-fishing equipment, but light tackle equipment is available. McCoy's is also fully equipped for deep-sea fishing; ice, bait, and tackle are provided.

Southern Cross Club
☎ (345) 948-1099; fax (345) 948-1098
Three vessels, 16 to 24 feet in length, take groups
of two, three or four deep-sea fishing. Full- and
half-day reef fishing also available.

On Wheels

 If you're just seeing Little Cayman as a day tripper,
consider a guided excursion with an island local. An
overview of Little Cayman's attractions is available
through Island Air and local guide Chip McCoy. The package
includes round-trip air, an island tour by car, snorkeling along
Bloody Bay Wall, and lunch at uninhabited Owen's Island. The cost
is US $170. Contact **Island Air** (☎ 345-949-5252).

The island has over eight miles of paved roads, but you'll find that
the unpaved sections are passable on mountain bikes. Many of the
accommodations include free use of bicycles, but rentals are available at McLaughlin's Enterprises, Little Cayman Beach Resort,
Pirates Point, and Paradise Villas.

Eco-Travel

Birding

 Birders enjoy the **Booby Pond Visitors Centre**, open
Monday through Saturday, 2-5. Operated by the National Trust, Booby Pond, the 1.2-mile-long brackish
mangrove pond is home to the Caribbean's largest breeding colony
of red-footed bobbies (*Sula Sula*) and a breeding colony of magnificent frigate birds. Approximately 30% of the Caribbean population
of red-footed boobies resides at this pond. Even without the help
of telescopes or binoculars, you can view the large white birds (or
their large, gray offspring) in the trees surrounding the brackish
pond. Over 7,000 of the birds make their home here. The visitors
center includes exhibits on the island's indigenous species, from
the common crab (*Eurytium limosum*) to the seed shrimp (*Ostracoda*)

to the pond's many resident birds. Friendly volunteers staff the center and welcome questions about the wildlife and island life.

The visitors center is part of the Booby Pond Nature Reserve, which has been designated an international RAMSAR site. For this recognition, which falls under the United Nations convention to protect wetlands for waterfowl habitats, a site must meet strict environmental criteria.

Occasionally, Booby Pond will smell like rotten eggs or sulfur. The odor is the result of hydrogen sulfide gas created from decomposing organic material in the pond. Under normal conditions, the gas is dissolved in the pond water, but when the water level drops occasionally the harmless gas is released into the air.

Admission is free, although donations are welcomed.

THE NATIONAL TRUST

The National Trust welcomes members and donations. Annual dues are US $30; membership includes updates on projects such as the Booby Pond. For information on the Little Cayman District Committee for the National Trust, contact Gladys Howard, Pirates Point Resort, ☎ (345) 948-1010.

Sightseeing

Most of the sights to be seen on Little Cayman are natural rather than man-made. Outdoor activities, especially scuba diving and fishing, draw most visitors.

Even non-birders enjoy the **Booby Pond Visitors Centre**. Ride a bicycle up to the center and enjoy an early morning on the covered porch and watch the show of birds. For a close-up look you can view the birds from two telescopes (available for use any time) on the visitors center porch. One telescope is positioned low, for use by those in wheelchairs. The boobies fly about 40 mph and nest in crude constructions made of rough sticks. After a look at the birds,

Little Cayman

step inside the visitors center to see exhibits on the birds of Little Cayman. A small gift shop sells locally made crafts and artwork.

For a look at Cayman's local turtles, stop by Bruce's **Turtle Nursery**. It's not the Cayman Turtle Farm, but that's part of its charm. Just park your car and follow the ropes back to the turtle tanks for a self-guided, free look at these marine creatures. Three tanks hold green sea turtles. The nursery is located next to Bluewater Divers.

Where to Stay

Small resorts, condominiums, and an efficiency apartment complex make up the accommodations offerings.

Rental Agency

Blossom Villas, ☎ (345) 948-1000, fax (345) 948-1001. $$. When you arrive on Little Cayman, your rental car will be picked up from the island's only agency: McLaughlin's. Well, that same agency also serves as the reservation service for several island condominiums, good choices for those seeking for seclusion and privacy.

Lighthouse Point Condos. $$. Two-bedroom (twin beds in upstairs room), one-bath units offer a seaside location, screened dining porch, and a sun deck with a sunset view. These units are one of the more popular budget choices on the island and include a full kitchen. Available through Blossom Villas.

Bloody Bay House offers two bedrooms, one bath, and breezy decks. This rental is a favorite with divers as it sits across the road from the Bloody Bay Wall. $$. Available through Blossom Villas.

South Side Cottage has two bedrooms, one bath, and a screened verandah. $$. Available through Blossom Villas.

Sunset Cottage is a two-bedroom, two-bath home located seaside. It includes a screened porch off the master bedroom and another off the living/guest bedroom. This unit sleeps six guests. $$$. Available through Blossom Villas.

Sunset Point Condo offers four units with screened porches. The two-bedroom, 2½-bath units are two-story and each has wonderful views. These units sleep six guests and have a full kitchen, dining and living room. $$$. Available through Blossom Villas.

All of these properties have fully equipped kitchen, air-conditioning, and private laundry facilities. Transfers from the airport are included. A 50% deposit is required.

> **TIP:** *Families who may be considering a stay in one of Little Cayman's condominium units will find that cribs are available at most properties. However, parents with infants should bring baby needs, including disposable diapers, formula, and baby food. Such items are difficult, if not impossible, to find on-island.*

Hotels & Resorts

Little Cayman Beach Resort, Little Cayman, ☎ (800) 327-3835 or 813/323-8727, fax 813-323-8827. $$$. Little Cayman's largest property is specially tailored for those who want luxury with their adventures. This two-story conch-shell pink resort overlooks a shallow area inside the reef on the south side of the island. Just outside the reef lie top scuba spots, accessible through Reef Divers, the on-site operator. Dive packages include one-tank dives ($35 for an afternoon dive, or $45 for a night dive). Other rates include $65 US for two-tank morning dives. Beginners can learn with a resort course or obtain open water certification. Underwater photographers can see their shots the same day; an underwater photo and video center has E-6 processing and rentals.

Non-divers also enjoy this resort for its laid-back atmosphere. Hammocks sway just yards from the shore; chaise longues line the freshwater pool just steps from the bar. Rooms have air-conditioning, balcony or patio, color TV, ceiling fan, private beach. New oceanfront rooms feature wetbars, microwaves, and coffee-maker. Facilities include a restaurant, bar, gift shop, freshwater pool, fitness center, hot tub. Double occupancy rates in high season for a three-night, pool-view room range from US $415 for a non-diver, MAP (breakfast and dinner plan) to $695 for a dive package, all-inclusive plan (breakfast, lunch, dinner, unlimited drinks). Packages are per person and include airport transfers, government tax and service charges.

Little Cayman

Condos Paradise Villas, ☎ (345) 948-0001, fax (345) 948-0002. $-$$ (kids under 12 stay free when sharing a room with parents). Next door to the Hungry Iguana restaurant (and just steps from Blossom Village), these cozy villas are perfect for those who'd like housekeeping facilities but the option of both a nearby eatery and a grocery store. The villas – two units to a cottage – lie right on the beach. Each includes two twin beds or one king, a futon that can sleep one adult or two kids, a back patio overlooking the sea, full kitchen with microwave, toaster and coffee-maker, and air-conditioning. There's also a swimming pool and nearby restaurant.

Dive rates are $35 for a one-tank dive and $85 for a three-tank dive.

Conch Club, ☎ (800) 327-3835, (345) 948-1033. $$$ (two-bedroom unit). Located just north of Blossom Village, this condominium and townhouse project is the island's newest development. The lemon-yellow units are excellent for several couples traveling together or for families. Divers find the Conch Club within walking distance of one of the island's best dive shops. For those who want to take it easy, the two-story condominiums are just steps from the powdery beach.

The 12-unit complex offers two- and three-bedroom units. Two-bedroom units, spanning 1,700 square feet, include one queen, two twins, and one double convertible bed, as well as 2½ baths. At 2,000 square feet, the three-bedroom units offer one queen, one double, and two twin beds, as well as three baths. All units have a fully equipped kitchen, living and dining room, laundry facilities, ceiling fans, daily housekeeping, and use of pool, Jacuzzi, and dock on the property.

Several meal plans are available for guests. Modified American Plan (MAP) includes breakfast and dinner daily and runs US $40 for adults, $10 for children 5-11 (children under 5 are free). Full American Plan (FAP) offers breakfast, lunch, and dinner daily; it is priced at $59 for adults and $28 for children. The all-inclusive plan, all meals and beverages, is priced at $84 for adults and $39 for children. Meals are taken at the Bird of Paradise Restaurant at Little Cayman Beach Resort, next door.

Guests at the Conch Club can also enjoy scuba diving at Little Cayman Beach Resort. Full equipment rental, diving courses, and underwater photography equipment is available.

Small Inns

Little Cayman Diver II, ☎ (800) 458-BRAC. $$ (all-inclusive). Well, it's not exactly a small inn, but this live-aboard operates much like one. Based off Little Cayman, the boat accommodates 10 passengers in five cabins, each with a private bath. PADI, NAUI, SSI, NASDS, and YMCA affiliated, this operator has been in business for 10 years. It has video rentals.

Pirates Point Resort, ☎ (345) 948-1010; fax (345) 1011. $$. Children under 12 stay free in a room with parents; the child's meal plan is US $50 per day. Children five and over are welcomed. This 10-room resort is a favorite with divers and it's easy to see why. Four dive instructors reveal the secrets of Bloody Bay Wall, from sheer cliffs to delicate sponges and coral formations.

Non-divers find plenty of activity (or non-activity, if they so choose) at Pirates Point as well. Owner Gladys Howard is the chairperson of Little Cayman's National Trust committee and active in eco-tourism. The lobby of Pirates Point is filled with nature guidebooks, and Gladys also has a nature trail guide and fishing guide to take visitors out for a day or half-day of fishing or birding.

The resort offers plenty of temptation to just laze away the day on the powdery white beach as well. Guest cottages are simple and light, decorated in Caribbean colors. Rooms include ceiling fans, tile floors, and private baths. Drinking water is produced by the resort's own reverse-osmosis plant.

After a day in the sun, guests can relax in the island's most unusual bar, furnished with artwork created by previous guests. (The grounds of Pirates Point also feature guest-donated artwork, charmingly produced out of everything from coconut shells to driftwood.)

But there's no doubt that dining ranks as one of the top attractions of Pirates Point. Along with her expertise in natural history, Gladys Howard is also a Cordon Bleu-trained chef. While guests may rough it during the day, at night they enjoy gourmet meals as elegant as those found at any of the Caribbean's finest resorts. Gladys boasts, "my kitchen never closes."

Little Cayman

An all-inclusive dive package is available, including a deluxe room with private bath, three gourmet meals daily (with wine), open bar with unlimited drinks, two boat dives daily, use of all dive equipment, airport transfers, use of bicycles, and hammocks, lounges, and beach towels. For non-divers, an all-inclusive package has all of the above except diving. Hotel tax and gratuity are not included.

Southern Cross Club, ☎ (800) 899-2582, (345) 948-1099; fax (345) 948-1098. Reservation office: fax (619) 232-5114. $$$. The Southern Cross holds the distinction as the island's first resort. Located along South Hole Sound, this resort was recently renovated. Today, five beachfront cottages offer 10 guest rooms decorated in island colors; each room has air-conditioning, ceiling fans, (no phones or TV) and plenty of water from the inn's own desalinization plant. Facilities include a freshwater swimming pool and outdoor bar.

Southern Cross has long been a favorite destination with Caribbean anglers. Both deep-sea and tackle fishing for bonefish, tarpon, and permit are offered here. The Southern Cross Club has a 24-foot deep-sea fishing boat and a resident fishing guide to make sure you'll return home with plenty of fish tales.

Three dive boats offer daily dives at this PADI and NAUI certified shop. This is now an IANTD Nitrox facility

If a day of diving and fishing leaves you hungry, that's no problem at this resort. One of the managers, Stephanie Shaw, is trained by the Culinary Institute of America and she oversees meals for both guests and day visitors alike.

Sam McCoy's Dive Lodge, ☎ (800) 626-0496, (345) 948-0026; fax (345) 948-0057. $$. One of the island's earliest accommodations remains one of its favorites, especially with divers and fishermen. Sam and Mary McCoy are longtime Little Cayman residents and their son, Chip, now operates a popular day trip service (see *Adventures* on Little Cayman).

Two dive boats, the 30-foot *Caymaniac* and the 28-foot *Caymanak*, transport divers to sites around the island. Anglers can head out aboard the 32-foot *Reel McCoy* deep-sea fishing boat.

Eight guest rooms greet visitors with rustic charm. Tucked beneath shady trees and always in sight of the deserted beach, the rooms feature private baths and air-conditioning. Guests can dine right on premises. Other facilities include a small freshwater pool with Jacuzzi jets.

The Village Inn, ☎ (345) 948-1069; fax (345) 948-0073. $. Located right in "downtown" Blossom Village, the Village Inn is the island's only motel-type facility. Eight units, each with air-conditioning and a fully equipped kitchen, are available on a daily, weekly, or monthly basis.

Where to Eat

To cut food costs, many guests on Little Cayman opt for buying a few groceries. The lone grocery store is the Village Square, next to the car rental agency. Open 9-1 and 4-6, Monday through Saturday, the store stocks a little of everything: housewares, bait and tackle, VCR rentals, medicines, and groceries.

A surprising number of resorts feature top-notch dining. Pirates Point showcases the talents of Cordon Bleu-trained owner-chef Gladys Howard and serves up gourmet cuisine; the Southern Cross Club features a Culinary Institute of America-trained chef. The island has only one stand-alone restaurant.

Hungry Iguana, ☎ (345) 948-0007, $-$$. The Hungry Iguana is near the airport. The namesake of the seaside eatery is an iguana often seen at the airport. To honor the hungry herbivore, the restaurant sports a 40-foot mural of the local lizard. Continental buffet breakfasts start the day; lunch and dinner feature jerk chicken, grouper sandwiches, prime rib, and burgers.

Shopping

No one ever said Little Cayman was a shopper's paradise. Don't look for duty-free bargains or anything resembling a good selection of merchandise of any type. You will find assorted small gift stores around the island, primarily at the resorts. At Little Cayman Beach Resort, Mermaids sells jewelry, Spanish coins, clothes, and gift items; the shop is open afternoons only Monday through Saturday. t-shirts and some souvenir items can be found at the grocery store and the small shop adjoining McLaughlin's rental agency in Blossom Village. A small gift shop at Pirates Point sells a variety of

Little Cayman

items, including a Little Cayman cookbook prepared by Gladys Howard for the National Trust.

Booklist

Bradley, P. *Birds of the Cayman Islands*. Italy: Caerulea Press, 1995.

Brunt, M.A., ed. *The Cayman Islands: Natural History and Biogeography*. Kluwer Academic Publishers, 1995.

Cancelmo, Jesse. *Diving Cayman Islands*. Aqua Quest Publications, Inc. 1997.

Cohen, Shlomo. *Cayman Diver's Guide*. Tel Aviv, Israel Seapen Books, 1990.

Fosdick, Peggy and Sam. *Last Chance Lost?* (story of the Cayman Turtle Farm). Naylor Publishing.

Henderson, James. *Jamaica and the Cayman Islands*. Macmillan Publishing Co., 1996.

O'Keefe, M. Timothy. *Sea Turtles: The Watchers' Guide*. Lakeland, Florida: Larson's Outdoor Publications, 1995.

Philpott, Don. *Cayman Islands*. NTC Publishing Group, 1996.

Pitcairn, Feodor U. and Hummann, Paul. *Cayman: Underwater Paradise*. Reef Dwellers Press, 1979.

Potter, Betty. *Grand Recipes from the Cayman Islands*. Cayman Islands: Potter Publications, 1985.

Proctor, George, PhD. *Flora of the Cayman Islands*, Balogh Scientific Books.

Raultbee, Paul G., comp. *Cayman Islands*. ABC-CLIO, Inc., 1996.

Roberts, Harry H. *Field Guidebook to the Reefs and Geology of Grand Cayman Island, BWI*. Atlantic Reef Committee, 1977.

Roessler, Carl. *Diving and Snorkeling Guide to the Cayman Islands*. Gulf Publishing Co., 1993.

Sauer, Jonathan D. *Cayman Islands Seashore Vegetation: A Study in Comparative Biogeography*. Books on Demand (University of California Publications in Entomology), 1982.

Wood, Lawson. *Dive Sites of the Cayman Islands*. NTC Publishing Group, 1997.

Index

Discover Hunter's Travel Guides

Hunter Publishing offers thousands of travel guides to suit all tastes and budgets. All books are profiled on our easy-to-navigate Web site, www.hunterpublishing.com, which has descriptions of each book, along with cover images and reviewer comments. You may order through the Web site with a credit card, or simply use it as a research facility to find out more about our books.

All other orders may be directed to Hunter Publishing, 130 Campus Drive, Edison, NJ 08818, ☎ 800-255-0343. Please include $3 shipping and handling.

Adventure Guide to the
Leeward
Islands

Anguilla, St. Martin/Sint Maarten, Antigua, Barbuda, St. Kitts & Nevis, St. Barths

The glorious white-sand beaches and azure-blue seas of the Leeward Islands beckon travelers from far and wide. Exotic tropical flowers and sparkling waterfalls add to their appeal. Indeed, the Leewards attract thousands of visitors annually. Few leave disappointed with their experience. The vast majority vow to return again and again.

Each of the islands in this chain has its own history, culture and ecology, offering a cultural mélange for those on an island-hopping vacation. Rainforest, beaches, wetlands, mangrove swamps and offshore shoals afford an unlimited variety of places in which to create your own adventure vacation.

The *Adventure Guide to the Leeward Islands* is THE ultimate resource if you're heading for some fun in the sun. Covering all the usual sites and attractions featured in other guidebooks, including historical forts, plantations and in-town places of interest, this *Adventure Guide* takes exploration a step farther. It leads you away from the tourist traps and into the heart of the island to discover hidden waterfalls, pure mountain streams and secret trails. In addition, you'll find an entire run-down on where to stay and eat, from five-star resorts to family-run B&Bs and from haute cuisine to roadside stands selling "the best BBQ chicken on the island."

Focusing on outdoor activities, the authors recommend local tour operators and adventure outfitters, with contact names and numbers.

320 pp, $16.95, 1-55650-788-7

C RUISING THE
C ARIBBEAN

2nd Edition

As pursers on a major cruise line, the authors of this book were constantly bombarded with the same questions: *Where's the nearest beach? Do I have to get a cab there? Do I have time to go shopping? Where are the best shops, anyway?* Tired of repeating the answers, Laura & Diane Rapp decided to write a book answering every question their passengers might have.

Cruising the Caribbean is a cruise ship passenger's bible, not to mention a purser's dream come true! With this guide you can be sure to see and do exactly what you want ashore, whether it's hiking in the rainforest, duty-free shopping, sipping piña coladas on the beach or taking in the town's historical sites. Detailed intineraries cover a wide range of interests in each port of call, with tips on who can lend a helping hand, transportation options, and personal recommendations based on first-hand experience. The Rapps' humorous writing style adds a flavor all its own, with a look at some of the most frequently asked – yet unbelievable – questions asked of a purser, such as *What do you do with the ice carvings after they melt?, Do these stairs go up or down?* or *What time is the midnight buffet?*

280 pp, $15.95, 1-55650-799-2

- ◆ Antigua
- ◆ Barbados
- ◆ Dominica
- ◆ Grenada
- ◆ Guadelo

- ◆ Martinique
- ◆ Puerto Rico
- ◆ St. Kitts & Nevis
- ◆ St. Lucia
- ◆ St. Maarten/St. Martin

- ◆ St. Thomas

Best Dives of the Caribbean

2nd Edition

- Anguilla, Antigua
  & Barbuda
- Aruba
- Barbados
- Belize
- Bonaire
- British Virgin Islands
- Cayman Islands
- Cozumel
- Curaçao
- Dominica
- Dominican Republic
- Grenada
- Guadeloupe
- Honduras
- Jamaica
- Puerto Rico
- Saba
- St. Eustatius
- St. Kitts & Nevis
- St. Lucia
- Sint Maarten/St. Martin
- St. Vincent &
  the Grenadines
- Tobago
- US Virgin Islands

The second edition of this best-selling scuba and snorkeling guide is packed with details on the best coral reefs and shipwrecks for every skill level. A "starfish" rating is applied to each and every site, with five stars indicating the very best in visibility and marine life.

Each destination chapter offers tips on when to go, what to pack and how to get there. Also covered are live-aboard accommodation options and motor yacht vacations, topside sightseeing and activities, restaurants, handicapped diving information and money-saving tour packages. Detailed maps of every island show the best dive and snorkel spots.

See mammoth rock formations, sunken ocean liners, a WWII military ship, a tugboat, car piles, light plane wrecks, enormous earthquake fissures, artificial reefs, mysterious white and blue holes teeming with sharks and rays, WWII bombers, monster anchors lost by galleons of the 1800s, cannons and much, much more!

384 pp, $18.95, 1-55650-798-4